HEEDING THE CALL

HEEDING THE CALL

Jewish Voices in America's
Civil Rights Struggle

Norman H. Finkelstein

The Jewish Publication Society

Philadelphia Jerusalem

5757 / 1997

Library of Congress Cataloging-in-Publication Data

Finkelstein, Norman H.
   Heeding the call: Jewish voices in America's civil rights
struggle / by Norman H. Finkelstein.
      P.   cm.
   Includes bibliographical references and index.
   Summary: Discusses the involvement of Jews in the African American
struggle for civil rights in the United States, from the first
settlers up to the 1990s.
   1. Jews--United States--History--Juvenile literature. 2. Afro-
Americans--History--Juvenile literature. 3. Civils rights workers--
United States--Juvenile literature. 4. Judaism and social
problems--Juvenile literature. 5. Afro-Americans--Relations with
Jews--Juvenile literature. 6. Antisemitism--United States--Juvenile
literature. [1. Afro-Americans--History. 2. Jews--United States--
History. 3. Civil rights workers. 4. Ethnic relations.]
I. Title.
E184.J5F484   1995
323. 1 '73--dc21   96-39693
                                                                         CIP
                                                                          AC

Designed and Typeset by Book Design Studio
Printed by

97 98 99 00 01 02
10 9 8 7 6 5 4 3 2 1

This volume is dedicated
in loving honor of the
Bar Mitzvah
of
Michael Scott Millner
Saturday, September 20, 1997
by
Goldie (ל"ז) and Abram Cohen
great grandparents
Betty Ann (ל"ז) and D. Walter Cohen
grandparents
Jane and Martin Millner
parents
Rachel and Lauren Millner
sisters

*For Jennifer, Jeffrey, Robert, Risa,
and especially, Rosalind. With love.*

CONTENTS

ACKNOWLEDGMENTS

I am grateful to the cheerful and competent librarians and archivists who guided me to valuable research material: Dr. Maurice Tuchman, Director of Library Services, Hebrew College, Brookline, Massachusetts; Ms. Virginia North, Archivist, The Jewish Historical Society of Maryland, Baltimore; Dr. Mayer Rabinowitz, Librarian, and Rabbi Jerry Schwarzbard, Special Collections Librarian, The Jewish Theological Seminary of America, New York; Ms. Cyma Horowitz, Library Director, American Jewish Committee, New York; Mr. Ronald J. Grele, Director, Oral History Research Office, Butler Library, Columbia University, New York; Ms. Holly Snyder, Archivist, and Ms. Michelle Feller-Kopman, Librarian, American Jewish Historical Society, Waltham, Massachusetts; Ms. Penina Abramson, YIVO Institute, New York; Ms. Margaret M. Jankowski, Archivist, Archives of Labor and Urban Affairs, Wayne State University, Detroit; Mr. Kevin Proffitt, Archivist, American Jewish Archives, Cincinnati; and the staffs of the National Archives and the Library of Congress (NAACP Papers), Washington; The Schomburg Center for Research in Black Culture, New York Public Library.

I also wish to thank Mr. Bruce Black, my editor at the Jewish Publication Society, my agent, Ms. Renee Cho and my wife, Rosalind, who each pleasantly suffers my idiosyncracies.

N.H.F.

INTRODUCTION

This book is not intended to be a comprehensive history of the African-American quest for freedom or the Jewish struggle for equality in the United States. Rather, it focuses on the long and difficult fight for civil rights through the words and actions of selected Jewish activists such as Levy, Einhorn, Wald, Spingarn, Wise, Rosenwald, and Heschel. Their contributions, largely unknown today, made a significant difference in securing rights for all.

Note

The use of various terms which identify African-Americans (e.g., Negro, Colored, or Afro-American) is in keeping with the authenticity of their usage in the respective time periods in which they appear.

1

NO JUSTICE, NO PEACE

"Hey Jew boy, you with that
  yarmulke on your head
You pale-faced Jew boy
  I wish you were dead."

From a guest on Julius Lester's radio show

It was an eerie moment. On stage, a fiery speaker electrified the crowd with a series of rapid-fire inflammatory questions. With equal fervor, hundreds of shrill voices responded to each question with the same single-word answer.

"Who caught and killed Nat Turner?"

"Jews!"

"Who controls the Federal Reserve?"

"Jews!"

"Who controls the media and Hollywood?"

"Jews!"

"You're not afraid to say it, are you?" the speaker asked.

"Jews! Jews!" came the now consistent reply.

This hateful scene did not take place in Nazi Germany in 1934. Instead, it took place in 1994 in Washington, D.C., at Howard University, the most prestigious of America's predominantly black institutions of higher learning.

Earlier the same year, readers of *The New York Times* were startled by a unique one-page advertisement. In bold, large type, the advertisement listed a vivid sampling of classic anti-Semitic statements. The advertisement was not sponsored by an obscure hate group but by the Anti-Defamation League (ADL) of B'nai B'rith, a leading Jewish organization dedicated to protecting civil rights. The ADL simply reprinted direct quotations from a rambling speech made at a New Jersey college by Khalid Abdul Muhammad, a leader of the Nation of Islam, a vocal and activist African-American organization. The Jewish organization voluntarily publicized the anti-Semitic remarks to plainly demonstrate the depth of mindless hatred. "Jews," Muhammad said, are "the blood suckers of the black nation."

"You call yourself Mr. Rubenstein, Mr. Goldstein, Mr. Silverstein," Muhammad continued, "because you been stealing rubies and gold and silver all over the earth." "We found out that the Federal Reserve ain't really owned by the Federal government...it's owned by the Jews...." Mr. Muhammad's racist charges, while shocking, were not unfamiliar. They were indicative of growing tensions between blacks and Jews in the United States.

On August 19, 1991, a mob of about twenty young men in the Crown Heights section of Brooklyn, New York, stopped an automobile and dragged the driver onto the street. There, amid shouts of "Kill the Jew!", they beat and stabbed to death Yankel Rosenbaum, a twenty-nine-year-old student. Rosenbaum's death was not accidental; he was murdered. "Nobody could have imagined," said Abraham Foxman, National Director of the ADL, "that in the streets of New York, this man would have met his death only because he was Jewish."

He was the innocent victim of a tragic incident which happened three hours earlier in which he played no part.

Crown Heights' population is 80 percent black. It is also the worldwide headquarters of the Jewish Lubavitch Hasidic movement. Members of that group comprise most of the remaining 20 percent of Crown Heights residents. Relations between Hasidim and blacks have been wary and tense. Most Hasidim, according to their religious beliefs and practices, are an inward people who try to avoid casual contact with the outside world. They prefer not to socially interact with others, Jewish or non-Jewish. People sometimes misunderstand this aloofness and feel slighted. A report by the American Jewish Committee explained that there were few open areas of communication to "dispel the prejudice and stereotypes that can run rampant between two vying communities that live in the same space, but in worlds apart."

At 8:20 P.M., a police-escorted motorcade was bringing Rabbi Menachem Schneerson, leader of the

Lubavitch Hasidic sect, home to Crown Heights from a visit to the cemetery where his wife was buried. The last car in the procession, trying to keep up with the convoy, ran through a red light, and hit two children on the sidewalk. Seven-year-old Gavin Cato was killed; his playmate badly injured. The driver of the car was a Lubavitch Hasid: the children were African-Americans.

Angry bystanders quickly gathered. While some tended to the children, others attacked the Hasidic driver who had to be rescued by police. "Get the Jews!" "Get the Jews!" came the shouts from the menacing crowd which soon overran the limited police presence. Fearful of stirring up further trouble, the mayor and police officials decided to keep a low profile. What ensued was three days of rioting during which Crown Heights' Jews were targeted for assault. Gangs of young blacks roamed the neighborhood without major police intervention, yelling, "Heil Hitler!" The neighborhood was "totally out of control," one police officer recalled. Terrified Jews hid in their houses, calling for police help that never came. "All you hear is shouting and screaming, thudding and glass breaking," one man told *The New York Times.*

Jews view what happened that day in Crown Heights as a modern day "pogrom" not dissimilar to the violent attacks on Jews and Jewish communities in Russia a hundred years earlier and Nazi Germany fifty years later. One woman later recounted, "I was a prisoner in my house for 72 hours. I was forced to hide in the bedroom with my six children. Our house was attacked twice, and the police wouldn't come to my family's aid. My children have been traumatized." At

4

Gavin Cato's funeral, inflammatory anti-Jewish eulogies echoed off signs which read, "Hitler didn't do his job."

Over a three-day period 65 civilians and 158 police officers were injured during rioting by angry blacks. Twenty-seven police cars were overturned, burned, or damaged. A young black man, Lemrick Nelson, Jr., was ultimately charged with Yankel Rosenbaum's murder.

When police arrested him, they found a bloody knife in his pocket. Tests proved the blood was Rosenbaum's. Nelson confessed to the police that he had killed the Jewish man. In spite of the evidence, a largely black jury later acquitted Nelson of the murder, further demoralizing the Jewish residents of Crown Heights.

The lightning rod for much of the anti-Semitic furor in America's black communities in the 1990s was Minister Louis Farrakhan, head of the militant Nation of Islam. The Nation of Islam is a black nationalist organization founded in 1930. Under the leadership of Louis Farrakhan, members continue to strongly believe in black self-reliance and separation from whites. Farrakhan's speeches, interviews, and public statements overflow with anti-Jewish rhetoric. He has referred to Judaism as "a gutter religion," called Israel "an outlaw state," and praised Hitler as "a very great man." Although viewed as an extremist by many, Farrakhan's teachings of self-reliance and pride found acceptance among many African-Americans including college students.

The unfounded accusations and incidents of racism outraged and confused Jewish-Americans. For decades,

5

Jews and African-Americans had worked together to combat the country's discriminatory laws and behavior. As anti-Semitic rhetoric in the black community heated up in the 1970s, 1980s, and 1990s, it became uncomfortably clear to many Jews that their long-standing partnership with the African-American community had faded away. What hurt Jews most of all was the reluctance of many mainstream black community leaders to publicly condemn the highly inflammatory anti-Semitism of Farrakhan and others. Those black leaders who did speak up were generally ignored.

Twisting history and inventing wild-eyed theories, extremist blacks blithely accused Jews of such evils as infecting African-American babies with AIDS and introducing drugs to youths in the black ghettos in order to control the African-American community. One of the most repeated lies was the charge that Jews were the instrumental force behind slavery in the United States. A simple study of the facts reveals the truth.

Few Jews engaged in the practice of slave trading. In 1830, only 1,500 Jews lived in the South and there were only "twenty-three Jews among the 59,000 slave owners owning twenty or more slaves and just four Jews among the 11,000 slave holders owning fifty or more slaves." Indeed, over 3,500 free blacks owned 12,000 slaves, more than the Jewish slave owners. Before the outbreak of the Civil War in 1861, the Jewish population of the United States had grown to approximately 150,000 people with 20,000 living in the South. Twenty-five percent of southern Jews—the same percentage as their white Christian neighbors—owned at least one slave.

Anti-Semitic remarks continued to undermine Jewish-black relations. In the 1984 presidential campaign, candidate Jesse Jackson created an uproar when he referred to Jews as "Hymies" and New York as "Hymietown." The insensitivity of his remarks demonstrated the pervasiveness of anti-Jewish feelings among many blacks.

Public opinion surveys conducted by the American Jewish Committee in 1992 and 1994 highlighted the growing rift between Jews and African-Americans. Polls indicated that anti-Semitic feelings were higher among African-Americans than other groups. Sixty-three percent of blacks polled said they believed Jews had too much power and influence. Fifty-four percent said Jews would choose money in a choice between people and money and 43 percent said Jews have too much control over business and the media.

A number of factors led to the breakup of the historic coalition of Jews and African-Americans. Jews and blacks in the North were urban dwellers. As Jews moved up the economic ladder out of the ghettos to the suburbs, blacks migrating from the South took their place. In 1969, Golda Meir, the prime minister of Israel, returned to the elementary school she attended as a child in Milwaukee, Wisconsin. There, a student chorus welcomed and enchanted her with a beautiful rendition in Hebrew of Hatikvah, the Israeli national anthem. The young singers, reflecting the changed racial composition of her old neighborhood, were African-Americans.

Left behind in the ghettos were small Jewish business and property owners. The relationship between Jewish merchants and poor blacks was not always pos-

7

itive. Black writer James Baldwin recalled, "The grocer was a Jew and being in debt to him was very much like being in debt to the company store. . . . We bought our clothes from a Jew and, sometimes, our second hand shoes. . . . "

In the 1960s, Jews became concerned about changing black views toward Israel. The image of Israel as a struggling democracy besieged by virulent enemies evolved into an image of Israel as a bastion of western colonialism which mistreated Arabs as downtrodden people of color.

A major turning point in Jewish-black relations was the Ocean Hill-Brownsville, New York teacher's strike in 1968. In an effort to improve education in the Ocean Hill-Brownsville section of Brooklyn, New York, the school board created a new school district under community control. Local community activists demanded a voice in educational control over the district schools, including the hiring and firing of teachers without regard to established regulations. The teacher's union objected. Ninety percent of New York City's public school administrators and teachers were white: two-thirds of them were Jewish. The high number of Jews was due to the high concentration of Jews in New York (approximately one-quarter of the population). Jews sought out careers in education and other public sector jobs since discrimination in the 1930s and 1950s locked them out of professional careers in the private sector. Large numbers of college-educated Jews became teachers and social workers. As African-Americans struggled for recognition and self-empowerment, Jewish teachers found themselves at the center of a no-win situation.

In the 1960s, an effort began to increase the number of black teachers in predominantly black communities of New York. Jewish teachers who had been working in those schools for years found themselves transferred and replaced. At issue was the civil service system which awarded jobs simply by merit without regard to race or religion. African-Americans argued that the system discriminated against them. A bitter two-month strike ensued. Anti-Semitic literature and picket-line chants soon turned the strike ugly.

Julius Lester, the black host of a radio talk show, encouraged an activist black teacher to read a particularly strident poem written by a student. The first few lines set the tone.

> *"Hey, Jew boy, with that yarmulke on your head*
> *You pale-faced Jew boy—I wish you were dead.*
> *I can see you Jew boy—no you can't hide*
> *I got a scoop on you—yeh, you gonna die..."*

Lester had hoped that the inflammatory words would disturb listeners enough to encourage the black community to cease the anti-Jewish nature of the controversy. Instead, the ferocity and hatred of the poem against Jews worsened the already tender situation. The ADL reported that "raw, undisguised anti-Semitism had reached a crisis level in New York City..."

Julius Lester was the son of a Protestant minister who became an activist for black rights in the South in the early 1960s. His great-grandfather, Adolph Altschul, was a Jew who emigrated from Germany to Pine Bluff, Arkansas. After the poem aired, Lester remarked, "As crude and obscene as the poem was, I heard in it an excruciating paroxysm of pain. It was pain expressed as anger at Jews...." With the memory of his Jewish great-grandfather haunting him, Julius Lester, by then a university professor, converted to Judaism in 1981. His journey from black-Christian activist to Jew is hauntingly described in his autobiographical book, *Lovesong: Becoming a Jew*.

Shortly thereafter, a special exhibit, "Harlem on My Mind," opened at New York's Metropolitan Museum of Art. The exhibit catalogue contained an inflammatory introduction written by a black high-school student. "Behind every hurdle that the Afro-American has yet to jump," she wrote, "stands the Jew who has already cleared it." Her words created a national furor.

Underlying much of the growing tension was the fight for affirmative action in America, and its related issue of quotas. Affirmative action, by which black Americans and other minorities were given preferential treatment in hiring, was implemented to make up for the country's past injustices to blacks. Rules were first instituted as part of the civil rights laws of the 1950s and 1960s. Goals or quotas, were set for businesses and schools. In 1961, President John F. Kennedy introduced affirmative action for all contracts with the United States government. The Equal Opportunity Act of 1972 mandated colleges, all governmental agencies, and private firms that received governmental contracts to increase the number of their women and minority employees.

Jews viewed affirmative action with apprehension. Numerical quotas for admission to American institutions of higher learning would restrict Jewish applicants to less than 3 percent of available spaces—the percent of Jews in America. Jews had fought hard to gain admission to prestigious universities by merit alone and constituted larger percentages in such professions as law, education, and medicine. Quotas would prevent the brightest and best of young Jews from professions they had worked so hard to enter. Jews vividly remembered the discrimination they had to overcome over the years to earn places in the educational and work world. While black groups supported quotas, most mainstream Jewish groups were opposed.

In 1970 and 1971, Marco De Funis, a Jewish student, applied for admission to the University of Washington Law School. He was rejected both years. Complaining that he would have been admitted without any hesitation on merit, but rejected because he was not black, De Funis sued. His case was the first of its kind to be heard by the United States Supreme Court. Because De Funis was allowed to enter the law school while the case made its way through the court system, the Supreme Court never ruled.

The Court did, however, rule in 1978 in the case of Allen Bakke, a white (but not Jewish) student who had unsuccessfully sought admission to the University of California Medical School at Davis. Bakke thought he would have been admitted had affirmative action not been in force. Ultimately, the Supreme Court, in a landmark 5 to 4 decision, sided with Bakke and ordered his admission to the medical school while at the same time upholding the use of race in university admissions. The decision basically banned the use of racial quotas. Many Jewish groups were relieved: they had backed Bakke by submitting legal briefs on his behalf to the Supreme Court. Black groups were incensed.

Thurgood Marshall, the only African-American member of the Supreme Court in 1978, was disappointed. In a memorandum to the other justices, he wrote: "The dream of America as the melting pot has not been realized by Negroes—either the Negro did not get into the pot, or he did not get melted down." During these years, the strategic alliance of African-Americans and Jews disappeared and with it the memory of a Jewish role in the historic civil rights struggle. "An understanding is expected of the Jew," black writer James Baldwin wrote, "such as none but the most naive and visionary Negro has ever expected of the American Gentile."

ONE FOR ALL

"Giving them [Jews] liberty, we cannot
refuse the Lutherans and Papists."

Governor Peter Stuyvesant

The first groups of Africans and Jews reached North America by ship in the 1600s, separately and under differing conditions. The first twenty Africans arrived in Virginia in 1619 as bound or indentured servants, to work for a predetermined time before receiving freedom. Other small groups followed. By 1654 when the first Jews arrived in New Amsterdam, the city we today know as New York, the black population there numbered about sixty. Along the Hudson River, outside of the settlement, large Dutch-owned farms were cultivated by black slaves. The Dutch mainly treated blacks humanely and with a sense of personal rights which vanished when the English took over the rule of New Netherlands in 1664. Under Dutch rule, a number of bound blacks were given their freedom along with large tracts of land, including much of today's Greenwich Village, where they built homes, farmed, and conducted their businesses. By the mid-1600s slavery was legalized in most English colonies in North America and the number of imported black slaves increased. At the same time there were a number of free blacks in the North who were either freed by their owners or who had bought themselves out of slavery.

By 1700 the slave population in North America was estimated at 28,000. Twenty-three thousand were located in the South where the expansion of agricultural businesses on vast plantations made slave labor a valuable economic necessity. By 1790, the number of blacks had grown to over 750,000, comprising nearly 20 percent of the total American population, then estimated at four million. The vast majority of them were slaves on southern plantations where, as a result of Eli Whitney's invention of the cotton gin in 1793, the need for slaves dramatically increased.

Less than 9 percent of American blacks were free, living mainly in the North where slavery fell out of favor. It was abolished in Rhode Island in 1774, in Vermont in 1777, and Massachusetts in 1783; other northern states followed. When the Declaration of Independence was written, the words "All men are created equal" did not apply to blacks. Although there was some anti-slavery activity in northern states during this period, most southerners considered their slaves not as fellow citizens but as property. Yet, in the

Revolutionary War, nearly 10,000 blacks served under George Washington to defeat the British.

Although northern states basically eliminated slavery within their borders, the framers of the United States Constitution had to consider other sectional and political needs. When the Constitution was adopted in 1787, it stated that the importation of slaves could not be prohibited before 1808, thereby allowing the slave trade to flourish in the South. In 1807, when President Thomas Jefferson officially signed the law abolishing the slave trade, it did not stop the continuation of slavery in the South.

In contrast, the Jewish population of North America in 1790 was estimated at 2,000. In 1654, the first Jewish settlers arrived in New Amsterdam on board the *Saint Catherine,* penniless but free. They were escaping religious persecution in Brazil which had been recaptured by the Portuguese from the Dutch. Their welcome by Governor Peter Stuyvesant and the leaders of Dutch New Amsterdam was less than cordial. Stuyvesant immediately wrote to his directors in Holland objecting to the newcomers and asking permission to prohibit any further Jewish arrivals. The Jews, Stuyvesant said, were "repugnant" and a "deceitful race" and should not be "allowed further to infect and trouble this new colony." "Giving them liberty," Stuyvesant argued, "we cannot refuse the Lutherans and Papists." Stuyvesant said he "preferred Negroes before Spaniards and unbelieving Jews."

But the refugees intended to stay and sought the support of other Jews in Holland, some of whom were shareholders in the Dutch West Indies Company, the owners of New Amsterdam. The company sent a message to Governor Stuyvesant which clearly stated, "These people may travel and trade to and in New Netherlands and live and remain there, provided the poor among them shall not become a burden to the Company or to the community, but be supported by their own nation."

Those first twenty-three Jewish settlers were not content to lead their lives according to selective rights handed to them. From the beginning they insisted on and ultimately received the same rights and benefits accorded to other residents. Leading their fight for

The first Jewish settlers arrived in the United States in 1654. They faced an uphill battle against discrimination. (New York Public Library Picture Collection)

equal rights was the fearless and outspoken Asser Levy, one of the original twenty-three Jewish travelers on the *Saint Catherine.*

Levy, impoverished upon arrival, was stubborn and proud. He eventually succeeded in obtaining permission to become a butcher with a provision which did not require him to sell pork products in respect of his religious beliefs. His determined fight for equal rights did not make him unpopular among many of his Christian neighbors. They respected his integrity and often turned to him for advice and help.

Because the small colony was in constant danger of attack, every able-bodied man over the age of sixteen was required to serve in the militia. When the question arose, "Shall the Jews be enlisted?", Stuyvesant and the Council responded. "That owing to the disgust and unwillingness of the militiamen to be fellow soldiers...Jews cannot be permitted to serve as soldiers, but should be exempt." Instead, the Council ruled, Jews would be required to pay a special monthly "contribution."

Most Jews grumbled and complained among themselves. Asser Levy decided to take action. He refused to pay the unfair tax and on November 5, 1655, he and Jacob Barsimson, another Jewish settler, presented a petition to the Council. The petition asked that they both be permitted to stand guard duty like other citizens of New Amsterdam or be excused from paying the unfair monthly tax. Their request was denied with the added message from the Council that if they were not happy, they could "depart whenever and whither it pleases them." Shortly thereafter, perhaps due to another successful appeal to Holland, Levy began to stand guard with his neighbors.

When Stuyvesant and the Council decided to repair and strengthen the protective wall around the settlement, all residents of New Amsterdam were asked to contribute funds. No one begrudged the need for the wall which protected them all. The Jewish residents, however, were singled out for larger "voluntary" contributions. Although they constituted only one-thirtieth of the total population, their "voluntary contribution" for the wall was one-twelfth of the total.

Ignoring the order from the Directors in Holland permitting Jews to freely "travel and trade," Stuyvesant prevented Jewish merchants from trading elsewhere in New Netherlands. On November 29, 1655, a petition signed by Abraham de Lucena, Salvador Dandrada, and Jacob Cohen requested permission to trade, like other residents, anywhere within New Netherlands, the province of which New Amsterdam was a part. The Council responded negatively, as expected.

When one of the Jewish settlers tried to purchase a house, that right was also denied. In response, they submitted a clearly detailed list of their grievances to Stuyvesant and the Council. One hundred and twenty years before the Declaration of Independence, they called for no taxation without representation. "If like other burghers, they must and shall contribute, [Jews must] enjoy the same liberty allowed to other burghers ...in trading...as in the purchase of real estate."

The Directors in Holland were also losing patience with the rulings of Stuyvesant and the Council and responded strongly. "We have here seen and learned with displeasure, that your Honors have forbidden [members of the Jewish nation] to trade...and also the purchase of real estate...and we wish that this had not occurred but that your Honors had obeyed our orders which you must hereafter execute punctually and with more respect."

Each new argument brought the Jews closer to obtaining full civil rights. One final hurdle remained—full citizenship with the right to vote. On April 11, 1657, Asser Levy appeared in court with a request to be granted full "Burgher"—or citizenship rights. Consistent to the end, the Council automatically denied Levy's claim. In response, other Jewish residents of New Amsterdam submitted a supporting petition on behalf of Levy and themselves. "Our Nation, as long as they have been here, have, with others, borne and paid, and still bear, all Burgher burdens...we, therefore, reverently request your Noble Worships to please not exclude nor shut us out from the Burgher right, but...to give us the customary Burgher certificate." Finally, on April 20, 1657, Peter Stuyvesant reluctantly recognized the claim and granted full rights of citizenship to the Jewish residents of New Amsterdam. Within the short space of three years, led by the activism of Asser Levy, the Jews of New Amsterdam rose from the status of unwelcome refugee to that of equal citizen.

During that struggle for recognition, Levy did more than gain equal rights for himself and the small group of Jewish refugees. As an outsider in a small settlement he risked social and economic isolation by his outspoken demands for equality. He set the scene for an America where, years later, determined individuals could fight for rights and freedom for all citizens.

The America of Levy's time and the colonial period which followed experienced a rapid growth in the number of black slaves. By the middle of the eighteenth century, black slavery was a fundamental part of the national economy. The slave trade between North America and Africa involved many people of many nationalities and religions on both sides of the Atlantic. The census of 1839, for example, discovered that over 3,500 blacks, mainly in southern states, owned slaves. In contrast, the role played by Jews (who were an almost immeasurable minority of Americans) in the slave trade was inconsequential. The noted historian, Jacob Marcus, wrote in *The Colonial Jew* that Jewish businesses imported less than 2 percent of black slaves to America. Jewish involvement paled in comparison to the involvement of Muslims, Protestants, and Catholics.

As more Jews migrated to America they tended to adopt the cultural ways of the established white community. New arrivals busied themselves with earning a living, raising families, and simply surviving in an alien land with alien customs. Jews remembered their unfavorable treatment in Europe and tended to keep a low profile and follow the practices and thoughts of their Christian neighbors. In the North, they were largely opposed to slavery. In the South, Jews owned slaves in the same proportion as their southern white Christian neighbors. By the middle of the eighteenth century, slavery played a key role in the South's developing economy. There were slaves in all thirteen colonies. Yet, by the time the Civil War erupted in 1861 over 90 percent of blacks were located in the South, most as slaves on large plantations.

The Jews who came to America had experienced rampant discrimination in Europe. In western Europe they were granted legal equality with their Christian neighbors only after the French Revolution of 1789. But the granting of legal rights could not erase centuries of anti-Semitism, even in the New World which offered hope of a better life but where Jews kept a wary eye open for signs of any reemergence of anti-Jewish sentiment.

Yet even in the New World, beginning with the experience of Asser Levy and the first Jewish community, Jews continued to face a series of discriminatory legal attempts to restrict their rights. Many colonies did not make Jews welcome. Jews faced residency bans, restrictions on businesses, home ownership, and citizenship. A request by Jewish merchants of Newport, Rhode Island for citizenship was rebuffed by the leaders of the colony since "no person who does not profess the Christian religion can be admitted free of this colony." Until 1868, Jews and Catholics in North Carolina were prohibited from holding political office. It was not until 1876 that similar rules in New Hampshire were finally eliminated.

With the passage of time, Jews gradually gained acceptance. With independence from England, the United States Constitution guaranteed their rights as citizens. Article VI of the Constitution guaranteed that "no religious test shall ever be required as a qualification to any office or public trust under the United States." While Jewish citizens could hold any federal office, including the presidency, barriers to full equality were not completely eliminated. In Maryland, where about 150 Jews lived in 1818, a bill was filed in the state legislature to "extend to those persons professing the Jewish religion, the same privileges that are enjoyed by Christians." It was not the first attempt at equal rights for Maryland's Jews that failed.

Beginning in 1797, Jewish citizens of Maryland had regularly petitioned their legislature for equal status "on the same footing with other good citizens." In effect, Jews were ineligible for any state public office because the Maryland Constitution required officeholders to legally declare "belief in the Christian religion." Since Jews could not assume that oath, they were not eligible to serve in the state militia, practice law, or hold any state government appointments. To right that injustice, a Presbyterian member of the legislature, Thomas Kennedy, filed the 1818 bill "To extend to the sect of people professing the Jewish Religion, the same rights and privileges that are enjoyed by Christians."

"There are not Jews in the country from whence I came nor have I the slightest acquaintance with any Jew in the world," the Scottish-born Kennedy told his colleagues. He simply believed that religion was "a question which rests, or ought to rest, between man and his Creator alone."

An article in a magazine of the time supported passage of the bill "to exonerate this persecuted sect from the odious restrictions which our *incomprehensible* constitution imposes upon them...Let us do our duty and place them upon an equality with ourselves." But opposition was rampant. Year after year the bill was defeated. In 1823, a "Christian Ticket" organized and defeated Kennedy at election time by a margin of 2 to 1. His opponent stated that the bill was an "attempt to bring into popular contempt the Christian religion... Preferring as I do Christianity to Judaism, Deism, Unitarianism or any other sort of new fangled ism...."

Kennedy was re-elected in 1824, the same year in which he finally succeeded in getting the "Jew Bill" passed. It went into effect in 1826 and later that year two Jews were elected to the Baltimore City Council. "They are the first Jews ever elected by the people to office in Maryland," a magazine explained, "being until lately denied the right of citizenship by the court and the state."

While Jewish Americans began to enjoy their long sought recognition as fully equal citizens of the United States, the situation of African-Americans worsened.

SPEAKING UP

"Is slavery a moral evil or not?"

Rabbi David Einhorn

Opposition to slavery developed slowly. In 1775 Benjamin Franklin founded the Society for Promoting the Abolition of Slavery. His goal was praiseworthy but premature. An activist anti-slavery movement did not have much impact before the 1830s when abolitionist societies were established in Boston and Philadelphia. Their activism went beyond speechmaking and pamphleteering to include an organized method of helping slaves escape their fate—The Underground Railroad. A network of brave "conductors" led escaping blacks through perilous routes to relative safety in the North and in Canada. Historian John Hope Franklin stated that "perhaps nothing did more to intensify the strife

between North and South [and demonstrate the]...
determination of abolitionists to destroy slavery, than
the underground railroad." The activity of the underground railroad only "intensified the resentment that
the South felt toward outside interference...."

Although many individuals in the South opposed
slavery, the anti-slavery movement was centered in the
North. By the 1850s the words and deeds of the abolitionists led to inevitable confrontations between
North and South. Although the number of committed
abolitionists was small, thousands of people were
sympathetic to the cause. With the publication of Har-
riet Beecher Stowe's *Uncle Tom's Cabin* in 1852, anti-
slavery feelings intensified, much to the dismay of
many southerners.

White activist William Lloyd Garrison of Boston
founded the widely read abolitionist newspaper, *The
Liberator,* in 1831. He took a militant stand against
slavery and became the nation's leading advocate of
nonviolence to achieve the abolition of slavery. "I am
in earnest," he wrote, "I will not equivocate—I will
not excuse—I will not retreat a single inch—AND I
WILL BE HEARD." In an article he wrote for *The Liberator* in 1838, Garrison compared the plight of
African-Americans to the situation of Jews. "The Jews
in Europe," he said, "were for a long time in a similar
situation being despised and abused from the mere cir-
cumstance of their descent and religion. The prejudice
against the Jews, though very much abated, continues
even at the present time."

The Quakers were the first group to adopt an anti-
slavery position and members of that religion took an

early leadership role in the abolition movement. Other Christian religious groups followed. American Jews, as a group, never took a stand on slavery. Not that most Jews outside the South supported slavery— far from it. But the number of Jews in the country was small and scattered and there was no central Jewish authority in the United States as there had been in the European countries from which they came. Each congregation was free to adopt its own practices and sentiments. Although many Jewish religious leaders of the time shared anti-slavery opinions, they viewed the Christian-oriented abolitionist movement with suspicion and kept their distance. A report to the 1853 meeting of a leading anti-slavery society accurately described Jewish attitudes.

> *The Jews of the United States have never taken any steps whatever with regard to the Slavery question. As citizens, they deem it their policy "to have every one choose whichever side he may deem best to promote his own interests and the welfare of his country...."*

> *The objects of so much mean prejudice and unrighteous oppression as the Jews have been for ages, surely they, it would seem, more than any other denomination, ought to be enemies of* caste, *and friends of* universal freedom.

Allied with those opposing slavery in nineteenth-century America were people working to obtain equal rights for women. Fighters for both causes frequently

27

overlapped. They organized meetings throughout the country and delivered thousands of speeches to sway public opinion. One renowned fighter for the rights of women and slaves was Ernestine Rose, a Polish immigrant and the only activist Jewish female abolitionist. In spite of her accented English, she soon became a much sought after speaker. This was a time for great debate on the major issues that divided America, slavery and women's rights. Abolitionists, feminists, and their opposers traveled the country to speak, debate, and encourage support. At an 1852 women's rights convention, Ernestine Rose proudly proclaimed, "I am an example of the universality of our claims: for not American women only, but a daughter of poor crushed Poland, and the downtrodden and persecuted people called Jews....I go for emancipation of all kind—white and black, man and woman. Humanity's children are, in my estimation, all one and the same family." Her passion was inspired by the words and deeds of the prophets of ancient Israel. Like Rose, they confronted injustice directly without fear or timidity. One admirer said, "Her eloquence is irresistible." But her thoughts on universality did not win over everyone who met her. One clergyman, highly annoyed at Rose and her message, bluntly dismissed her as "a female, born of Jewish parents in Poland."

The major argument used by Rose and other abolitionists was that slavery was contrary to the teachings of the Bible and the principles upon which America was founded. "All men are created equal," they forcefully argued, did apply to blacks. Rather than risk a divisive fight between slave-holding and non-slave-

Ernestine Rose. (Library of Congress)

holding states, certain political accommodations were made in Congress which intensified emotions but delayed armed confrontation. When Missouri, a territory with a large number of slave holders, applied for admission to the Union as a slave state in 1818, bitter conflict arose and Congress did not admit Missouri. A year later, Alabama was admitted as a slave state, resulting in an equal number of slave and free states. Then, Maine applied for statehood as a free state, thereby breaking the balance. In response, Congress created The Missouri Compromise of 1820. Maine was admitted as a free state and Missouri as a slave state with the added provision that no new slave states would be established north of Missouri's southern boundary along a latitude of 36 degrees 30'.

But the country continued its westward expansion. In 1854, Congress effectively repealed the Missouri Compromise with the Kansas-Nebraska Act thereby opening a new controversy. Settlers in the Kansas and Nebraska territories were left to decide the question of slavery. The process was rent by violence as armed groups of pro-slavery and anti-slavery settlers overran Kansas, rigged elections, and attacked each other. "Bloody Kansas" found itself embroiled in political and violent conflict that ultimately led to the Civil War.

Taking the law into his own hands, abolitionist John Brown, who considered himself on a mission from God, gathered a small group of like-minded individuals, including his own sons, committed to the use of violence to achieve freedom for slaves. Brown, who was born in 1800, became committed in the 1850s to ending slavery. He moved to Kansas where pro- and anti-slavery forces were linked in violent battle. Fighting with Brown through Kansas were at least three Jews including August Bondi, a young immigrant from Austria with a strong belief in equality. Bondi later said that as a Jew "I had a duty to perform, to defend the institutions which gave equal rights to all beliefs." "I am most anxious for a strenuous life," Bondi wrote, "I was tired of the hum-drum life of a clerk. Any struggle, any hard work would be welcome to me. I thirsted for it, for adventure." Riding with John Brown through

Kansas, young Bondi saw his share of action under fire fighting the pro-slavery "Border Rebels." Bondi described his experience with John Brown as follows: "We were united as a band of brothers.... He constantly preached anti-slavery. He expressed himself to us that we should never allow ourselves to be tempted by any consideration, to acknowledge laws and institutions to exist as of right, if our conscience and reason condemned them."

Bondi did not follow John Brown to Harpers Ferry, Virginia. There, in October, 1859, Brown, his sons, and a small group of dedicated followers seized the United States Arsenal and its store of guns and ammunition and waited for the hundreds of southern slaves they expected to join them in an armed rebellion against slave owners. The slaves never came. United States Marines under the command of Robert E. Lee did. Brown was put on trial for treason and hung. In death, he became a folk hero for abolitionists. When the Civil War broke out, Union soldiers sang as they marched, "John Brown's body lies amouldering in the grave, but his soul goes marching on!"

With the election of Abraham Lincoln as President of the United States in November, 1860, the country found itself in a desperate situation. The divisions between slave and free states were at the breaking point. On December 17, 1860, South Carolina seceded from the Union, soon followed by other states bordering the Gulf of Mexico. On February 9, 1860, Jefferson Davis was elected president of the Confederate States of America.

In a last gesture of reconciliation before the inauguration of the country's new leader, President James

Buchanan proclaimed a national fast day for January 4, 1861, to "mobilize national sentiment against secession." People concerned with the fate of the Union gathered in houses of worship. Perhaps the most widely reported sermon of the day was delivered by Rabbi Morris J. Raphall of Congregation B'nai Jeshurun in New York City. The rabbi had already achieved a reputation as a dramatic orator and writer. He had the distinction of being the first Jewish clergyman to deliver an opening prayer for a session of the United States Congress (February 1, 1860).

His National Fast Day sermon was titled, "Bible View of Slavery." It was reprinted in major newspapers in both the North, where it shocked and disappointed readers, and the South, where it was viewed with satisfaction. "Slavery has existed since the earliest time," the rabbi intoned. "Slave holding is no sin," he argued, since "slave property is expressly placed under the protection of the Ten Commandments... when it is commanded that the Sabbath of the Lord is to bring rest to ... 'Thy male slave and thy female slave.' (Exodus 20:10)."

Raphall challenged the abolitionists. "How dare you denounce slave holding as a sin? When you remember that Abraham, Isaac, Jacob, Job—the men with whom the Almighty conversed, with whose names he emphatically connects his own most holy name, and to whom He vouchsafed to give the character of 'perfect, upright, fearing God and eschewing evil' (Job 1:8)—that all of these men were slave holders, does it not strike you that you are guilty of something very little short of blasphemy?" Pro-slavery people were delighted with the rabbi's arguments. It was clear that the biblical view of slavery, as interpreted by the best-known rabbi in America, supported their cause.

The Jewish population of the United States in 1850 numbered less than 200,000. Considering that the Jewish population in the United States a decade earlier had been around 50,000, the jump in numbers was indeed dramatic. The majority of the recent Jewish immigrants were mainly from German-speaking countries of Europe, part of a larger wave of German immigrants who flooded America during that period.

Since 1848, a year of upheaval marked by a series of European revolutions and economic catastrophes, disillusioned Jews had joined others in a massive migration to America. The large number of German-speaking Jews dramatically altered the fabric of Jewish life in America and left a significant mark on the larger society. They were the first Jews some Americans ever saw.

Starting out as peddlers, many of the new arrivals set out into America's uncharted frontier to sell their wares. Singly at first, and then in small groups, they settled in the remotest parts of the new country in cities such as Des Moines, Iowa; Pontiac, Michigan; and Abilene, Kansas. The businesses they founded and their later philanthropy and involvement in community life were legendary. Within a generation, Bloomingdale, Filene, Levi Strauss, and Guggenheim were household names.

The German Jews were the heirs of a relatively brief tradition of liberal ideas born in the French Revolution of 1789. Prior to the Revolution and its ideals of liberty, fraternity, and equality, European Jews were considered outsiders, subject to virulent discrimination, violence, and expulsions. In many European countries, Jews were geographically restricted. In Russia, for example, they lived in an immense area called the Pale of Settlement. In Western Europe they resided in much smaller areas of major cities known as ghettos. In the liberal atmosphere created by the French Revolution, a debate opened concerning the treatment of Western European Jews. "The Jews should be denied everything as a nation," a French leader argued, "but granted everything as individuals." No longer relegated to second-class status, Jews found themselves suddenly thrust into the world limelight.

In 1807, Napoleon assembled a convocation of Jewish lay and religious leaders to define the religious and civil status of French Jews. What emerged was a new self-image for Western Jews founded on religious and lifestyle reform. Although real emancipation took decades to implement, opportunities in business, education, and the arts slowly opened up for the Jews. The result was two distinct Jewish populations in Europe: the assimilated Westernized Jews and the ghettoized Jews of Eastern Europe. In Germany, Jews made the most advanced changes in traditional religious practices and teachings to form a Judaism more compatible with the modern world. In so doing, they made it unnecessary for Jews to choose between their religion and their new assimilated lives.

The German Jews who began arriving in America in large numbers brought their teachings and ideas with them. They also brought the liberal religious practices

34

that evolved into Reform Judaism. It did not take long for Reform to flourish on American soil. In America each Jewish congregation was independent and not subject to the decisions of a central religious authority. The reforms appealed to the majority of Jews in America who wanted to fully participate in American society without the restrictions of traditional Judaism.

Democracy and freedom seemed to emerge at once on both sides of the Atlantic, yet with imperfect results. In Western Europe, the emancipation of the Jews steadily proceeded although not without problems. In America, George Washington was inaugurated as the country's first president, and the Bill of Rights, the first ten amendments to the Constitution, was adopted by Congress. It did not consider the rights of African-American slaves, who would not be emancipated until the Civil War.

At the same time that abolitionists were publicizing the harsh and inhuman treatment of African-American slaves, newly arrived Reform Jews remembered their own immediate pasts. In Europe, they too had experienced firsthand the results of a larger society questioning whether Jews were naturally inferior to non-Jews or if the ghetto environment caused the Jews to display "backward" social customs and traditions.

Many Reform Jews in America sympathized with the abolitionists. Their experiences as liberals in Europe, together with their belief that Judaism stood for social justice, aligned them with those who opposed slavery, though not many joined the actively Christian abolitionist groups. Nearly all the well-known Jewish abolitionists were Reform Jews. A

35

prominent exception was Rabbi Sabato Morais who later became one of the founders of Conservative Judaism in America. He "uttered burning words of protest against slavery on behalf of Orthodox Judaism, in spite of the pro-slavery sentiments of some of his congregation, who for a time even prevented him from speaking." These Jewish abolitionists, just like their Christian colleagues, were deeply affected by the American democratic spirit. The liberal European beliefs of the newly arrived German Jews coincided with the ethical nature of Christian abolitionists. "Humanity before all things," said William Lloyd Garrison—"before all books and before all institutions: and God in the soul is the only authority."

Perhaps the strongest reaction to Rabbi Morris Raphall's interpretation of the biblical view of slavery came from Rabbi David Einhorn, one of the best-known Jewish abolitionists. He was, as one of his students later remembered, "a very exceptional man, whose solemn gravity and intense fervor indicated a life steadfastly given to the spreading of his inmost convictions."

David Einhorn was born in Bavaria, Germany on November 10, 1809. He was ordained a rabbi at the age of seventeen. Trained in traditional Orthodox Judaism, he also studied philosophy and classics at German universities at Erlagen, Wurzburg, and Munich and became a strong advocate of reforming Judaism for the modern world. He served as rabbi for several German synagogues, ultimately moving to a synagogue in Budapest, Hungary. "Jews and Christians flocked to his temple where reason and common sense in place of creed and dogma were preached." Never afraid of controversy,

Einhorn continued to upset traditional Jewish religious leaders and governmental officials with his innovative attempts to modernize the practice of Judaism. He eliminated prayers that referred to a return to a Jewish state and the services in the ancient Temple in Jerusalem. He also substituted much of the Hebrew language in the prayer book with German.

Rabbi David Einhorn. (Maryland Jewish Historical Society)

Speaking at an 1845 rabbinic conference in Frankfurt, Germany, he eloquently made a case for the increased use of the German language in religious services. "As long as prayer was mainly the cry of the oppressed Jew, the scarcely intelligible Hebrew sufficed. Now people need prayer as the simple expression of their innermost thoughts, convictions and sentiments. This can only be attained through the mother tongue."

In 1855 Rabbi David Einhorn came to America to assume the pulpit at Baltimore's Har Sinai Congregation, one of the earliest Reform houses of prayer in the United States. Baltimore had the unenviable reputation of being a "mob town"—half-North and half-South—where citizens frequently took to the streets to vent feelings on the day's political issues. The years prior to the Civil War were particularly divisive as pro- and anti-slavery forces competed for support. Into this charged environment came Rabbi Einhorn, ready to take up the fight for freedom. Einhorn followed in the tradition of the ancient prophets of Israel who, ignoring personal harm, were stirred by a "flaming fire within" (Jeremiah 25:9) to speak out for justice. Rabbi Einhorn founded a German-language periodical on Jewish themes which he called *Sinai*. He used the pages of *Sinai* to speak against slavery, which he called "the cancer of the Union." "Does the Negro have less ability to think, to feel, to will? Does he have less of a desire to happiness? Was he born not to be entitled to all these?" "It is the duty of Jews," he wrote, "to fight bigotry since, for thousands of years, Jews have consciously or unconsciously fought for freedom of conscience."

In one of his earliest articles, Einhorn vigorously supported the founding of the Black Republican Party to combat slavery. "We cannot share the fears of those who think that the triumph of this party would lead to the dissolution of the Union...." As the debate intensified, so did Einhorn's anger. "Any Jew who lifts his hand against the Union is, as a Jew, to be considered equal to a parricide [the killing of one's father]."

It was in the pages of *Sinai* that Einhorn forcefully rebutted Rabbi Raphall's defense of slavery. Einhorn could not accept Raphall's literal interpretation of the Bible as representative of all Jewish thought in America. Einhorn insisted that just because a particular practice was condoned in the Bible it does not make it right for modern times. The real question, according to Einhorn, "simply is: Is slavery a moral evil or not?" "Does a disease...cease to be an evil on account of its long duration?" He forcefully argued that the spirit of Judaism, as opposed to its letter, demanded the abolition of slavery. "The Bible," he wrote, "merely tolerates this institution as an evil not to be disregarded, and therefore infuses in its legislation a mild spirit gradually to lead to its dissolution."

Einhorn's words were translated from German into English and reprinted in pamphlets and in several New York newspapers. Reaction was swift, and not unexpected. Abolitionists were reassured that Raphall's much-publicized view was not representative of all Jewish thought. Pro-slavery supporters in Baltimore discovered a new target for their hate and threats were made against Einhorn and his family. Jewish members of other Baltimore congregations publicly disassociated themselves from his leadership. As the country hovered between war and peace, everyone anxiously wondered what would happen next.

The question was answered on April 12 when Fort Sumter, at the entrance to the harbor of Charleston, South Carolina, was bombarded by Confederate artillery, signaling the start of the Civil War. At 4:30 A.M. the Union troops inside surrendered. On April 15, President Abraham Lincoln issued a proclamation calling out 75,000 militia. Four border states—Virginia, North Carolina, Tennessee, and Arkansas—seceded from the Union. The fifth, Maryland, did not secede but remained bitterly divided. Maryland was a crucial state.

A mob attack in Baltimore on federal troops led to the first bloodshed of the Civil War and days of rioting. (Maryland Jewish Historical Society)

Washington, D.C. was within its borders and it was an important rail transportation center linking the nation's capital with the northern states.

The first shot of the Civil War was fired at Fort Sumter. The first casualties of the war occurred in Baltimore a week later. The Sixth Massachusetts Regiment was first to heed President Lincoln's call for troops to defend Washington. Its eleven companies of soldiers—approximately seven hundred men—had been honored in Boston and cheered enthusiastically on a march down Broadway in New York City as they made their way to the nation's capital. At 11:00 A.M. on April 19, 1861, the train carrying the Massachusetts troops arrived at Baltimore's President Street Station.

The railroad cars were unhitched to be drawn on rails by horses through the streets of Baltimore to the Camden Street Station for the continuation of their trip to Washington. The sight of Union soldiers on the streets of Baltimore inflamed pro-slavery citizens. The first cars to pass were jeered and hooted with abusive language as angry crowds gathered along the route. Then, the tracks were blocked and the remaining soldiers were forced to disembark and form ranks for a march to the station. The angry crowd thickened and pressed upon the advancing troops. Soon, rioting broke out. A barrage of stones rained upon the soldiers, injuring several. Other rioters wrestled muskets from soldiers and fired into the rank of troops. Four Massachusetts soldiers fell dead during the march and over thirty were seriously injured. The order to return fire was finally given. Twelve citizens of Baltimore were killed and others wounded. Gradually, the soldiers forced their way through the hostile rioters and onto the Washington-bound train.

Rioting continued until martial law was imposed on May 13. Southern sympathizers set out on a reign of terror that included murdering pro-Union activists. The mobs attacked and burned homes and businesses. They destroyed the presses of opposing newspapers including the one belonging to the printer of Einhorn's magazine. The lives of Rabbi Einhorn and his family were in danger. More than any other clergyman in Baltimore, Einhorn had "repeatedly denounced slavery with a courage that was equaled only by his moving eloquence." Word had been passed to the rabbi that his name appeared on a list of people to be attacked. Young men of the congregation armed themselves and set up guard around the Einhorn home.

In spite of the danger, Einhorn was reluctant to leave his congregation. He knew, however, that if he remained, "at least a large portion of the members of the congregation would listen to my sermons only with trembling and anxiety over their own safety and mine." Einhorn recalled, "I was given the assurance that my congregation requested me to go away, for the time being, but that it would call me back at the proper time." Concerned about his frightened family's safety, Einhorn, his wife and children fled Baltimore on April 22 by horse and carriage to Philadelphia.

When order had been restored in Baltimore, the officers of Har Sinai sent a letter to Einhorn "longing for your return." The rabbi responded for assurance that the congregation was again ready to "listen fearlessly to the pure teachings from the mouth of its teacher." The answer from Baltimore was not reassuring. "It would be highly desirable, both for your own safety's sake and in consideration of the members of your congregation, if in the future the pulpit sermons should avoid touching on

Rabbi Einhorn's flight from Baltimore. (Maryland Jewish Historical Society)

exciting questions of the day...." "Having received this letter," Einhorn later wrote in *Sinai,* "I could not doubt for one moment which way I had to go....I had to choose between diminishing the truth and abandonment of the safety of the congregation." David Einhorn submitted his resignation from Har Sinai.

In a letter accepting the resignation, the congregation's secretary wrote, "The congregation is only asking you to be kind enough to correct the following sentence in the latest copy of *Sinai*: 'that my congregation had requested me' [to leave Baltimore] to 'that the congregation in all probability would not mind.'" Einhorn became rabbi of a Philadelphia congregation and continued to speak out against slavery and for the Union.

Not everyone was sad to see Rabbi Einhorn leave Baltimore. Rabbi Benjamin Illowy, of the Baltimore Hebrew Congregation, condemned Einhorn and defended slavery as "a divine institution."

A New York newspaper, *The Jewish Messenger,* accused Einhorn of forsaking the role of rabbi by "making the pulpit the vehicle for political invective." The article continued, "A minister has enough to do, if he devotes himself to the welfare of his flock; he can afford to leave politics to others. Let Dr. E[Einhorn]'s fate be a warning." Einhorn, never shy to express an opinion, responded that "these rabbis used Judaism to consecrate slavery and were guilty of placing economic motivations above ethical doctrines of humanity."

David Einhorn died in 1879. His son-in-law, Rabbi Emil Hirsch, himself a noted scholar, later wrote about Einhorn's contributions to end slavery:

Had his been the vernacular of the land he would have been mentioned alongside Garrison, Phillips, Parker, Beecher and the valiant champions of the rights of man and other men of the herald voice who stirred to heroic deed... the thousands who went out to die so that the Union might live... He was the Jewish American patriot.

TO HELP AND HEAL

"I really love people."

Lillian Wald

On January 1, 1863, President Abraham Lincoln issued the Emancipation Proclamation freeing "all slaves in areas still in rebellion." The historic moment was etched forever in the minds of the freed slaves. Years later, Booker T. Washington recounted the moment in detail. "My mother...leaned over and kissed her children. While tears of joy ran down her cheeks...the wild rejoicing on the part of the emancipated colored people lasted but a brief period."

After the Civil War, amendments to the United States Constitution quickly legalized the rights of former slaves. The Thirteenth Amendment abolished slavery; the Fourteenth stated that citizenship rights could not be abridged by any state; the Fifteenth guaranteed that no citizen's right to vote can be denied "on account of race, color, or previous condition of servitude." In 1866, the United States government established the Freedmen's Bureau to help the former slaves make the transition to full citizenship and economic independence. Agents provided food, shelter, federal protection, and guidance while helping to build churches, businesses, and schools. Twelve black colleges such as Fisk University in Nashville, Tennessee, Hampton Institute in Virginia, and Tuskegee Institute in Alabama were founded under Freedmen's Bureau auspices.

It did not take long for the initial joy of emancipation to turn to anxiety. Former slaves, unprepared for freedom, found themselves without homes, jobs, and hope. Hunger and disease were common. Within two decades of the Emancipation Proclamation, the promises of freedom and equality made to the slaves were not fulfilled. Although legally free, they were no better off than they had been prior to the Civil War.

Southern legislatures attempted to deny former slaves their new freedoms by enacting a series of "Black Codes" that severely controlled the social, economic, and political lives of blacks. The Codes limited legal occupations of freed slaves to that of farmer and servant, then declared that any freed slaves without lawful employment were vagrants and subject to arrest. If they could not pay the unusually high fine, they "shall be hired out by the sheriff" to any white person. Many blacks had no choice but to return to work their former master's land as sharecroppers, binding "Negro families to the land and to white landowners almost as effectively as had slavery."

Under federal authority after the war, a period of Reconstruction attempted to fill the leadership vacuum created by the disappearance of civil authority in the South. Reconstruction attempted to restore the South's relations with the Union. The South suffered from massive economic and political problems. A major issue was the status of former African-American slaves whose new rights as full citizens were not welcomed by most southern whites. As new voters, freed slaves controlled the outcome of many southern state elections. Blacks were elected to numerous state and federal positions including the United States Senate and House of Representatives. The political gains made by blacks were short-lived. Union troops were withdrawn from the South in 1877 and power gravitated back to the states and local governments. By the 1890s, most of the rights blacks had gained were sharply diminished, including the right to vote. Beginning in Mississippi in 1890, literacy tests, poll taxes, and other requirements for voting were instituted as ways of excluding blacks from the ballot box. In 1964, the United States Supreme Court declared that the poll tax, which required a payment from every adult in order to vote, was unconstitutional. The Ku Klux Klan, founded in 1868, intimidated blacks and kept them away from the ballot box. Its white-hooded members struck terror throughout the South as violence against blacks became a way of life.

Restrictive "Jim Crow" laws further weakened the status of blacks, marking them as second-class citizens. The phrase "Jim Crow" was used to describe the segregation of African-Americans. It originated in a popular song in early nineteenth-century minstrel shows in which white entertainers blackened their faces and performed stereotyped imitations of blacks in song and dance. Blacks were segregated from whites in nearly all public places, from trains and buses to schools and water fountains. When blacks turned to the courts to right these wrongs, the response only solidified segregation in the United States for an additional fifty years. In 1896, the Supreme Court ruled in Plessy v. Ferguson in an 8 to 1 decision that segregation by race did not automatically mean racial discrimination. "Separate but equal"—the complete separation of the races—became a way of life in the South into the middle of the twentieth century.

Violence and the threat of violence were used to intimidate blacks and "keep them in their place." The white-hooded members of the Ku Klux Klan expanded on their hatred of blacks to include Jews and Catholics as well. The ultimate violence upon black men was murder by lynching. The hanging of blacks by white mobs became a near epidemic in the United States. From 1882 to 1927 over 3,500 lynchings took place without government intervention. Having witnessed a brutal lynching in Arkansas, a citizen appealed to President William McKinley, "Please, if possible do something for us." The plea was ignored.

While conditions worsened for African-Americans, discrimination against Jews intensified as the tiny Jewish population in the United States began to grow in size and prominence after the Civil War. Because of

50

harsh conditions experienced by Jews in Europe, life in America offered greater opportunities. By the 1870s, many children of German-speaking Jewish immigrants had become successful in business and the professions; a handful were philanthropists, endowing large sums of money for public benefit. As Jews became more conspicuous, others began to view them as social and economic threats. The result was the beginning of a period of unprecedented anti-Semitism in America. Like African-Americans, American Jews faced housing restriction covenants, employment bias, educational discrimination, and violence.

For several summers, Joseph Seligman, a well-known banker, friend of Abraham Lincoln, and leader of the American Jewish community, brought his family on vacation to the Grand Union Hotel in Saratoga Springs, New York. On arriving by carriage in June, 1877, Seligman was surprisingly denied entry. The owner had issued orders that "no Israelite shall be permitted in the future to stop in the hotel." "Outrage in Saratoga" was the headline in *The New York Times.* While politicians and clergy denounced the discrimination, Jews throughout the country found themselves barred from jobs in major industries, hotels, social clubs, and private schools. "Hebrew patronage not solicited" was a polite way of announcing that Jews were not allowed. Major universities, such as Harvard and Columbia, introduced quota systems limiting the number of Jewish students accepted for admission. Restrictive covenants prevented Jews from finding homes and apartments in desirable sections of major American cities.

However, it was an event that happened in a little Russian town in 1903 that shocked the world. To our modern world numbed by the horrors of the Holocaust, Rwanda, and Bosnia, what happened in Kishinev seems almost unimportant. Yet, to the world of that time, events there had the same notoriety as Auschwitz has now. In a particularly brutal pogrom, nearly fifty Jews were killed and thousands more savagely attacked. Women were raped and children were beaten. Jewish property was destroyed. The attacks took place during the Easter weekend, a traditional time for anti-Semitic attacks in Russia. But the pogrom was not totally religious in nature. It was well-planned and directed by Russian government officials partially as a warning to all Jews in Russia that anti-Semitism there would only worsen. The entire civilized world was shocked. There was universal condemnation of Russia for the pogrom and the continued harsh treatment of Jews. In the United States, a petition denouncing the massacre was signed by many congressmen and senators and forwarded to the Russian government by President Theodore Roosevelt. The Russians were genuinely surprised at this hostile reaction. Why should anyone care about the Jews?

In response to the violence against Jews in Russia, a number of prominent Jewish Americans, including Louis Marshall, a noted lawyer; Jacob Schiff, a financier; Cyrus Sulzberger, publisher of *The New York Times*; and Julius Rosenwald, the president of Sears, Roebuck and Company, formed the American Jewish Committee in 1906. The Committee was the country's first civil rights organization formed to "take concerted action against the constant and ever increasing efforts to traduce the good name of the Jew." Although initially dedicated to safeguarding the civil rights of Jews in Russia, its work broadened to include improving the legal and social conditions of Jews and other American minorities.

Louis Marshall, speaking in 1911, explained that the fight for Jewish rights was really a fight for the rights of all Americans. "It is not the Jew who is insulted; it is the American people. And the finding of proper remedy against this degradation is not a Jewish but an American question. ... I should deplore the day when there should ever arise a Jewish, a Catholic, or a Protestant question in the United States. We can never suffer any question here concerning individual rights but such as relates to the entire American People."

Louis Marshall was born in 1856 in Syracuse, New York. His parents, German-Jewish immigrants, provided him with a traditional Jewish upbringing and encouraged his participation in Jewish organizations. A graduate of Columbia University Law School, he became a well-known lawyer. In New York City, where he lived and worked, he served as president of Temple Emanu-El. Concerned with the increasing violence against the Jews in Russia, he, together with a group of other influential Jewish leaders, founded the American Jewish Committee. In 1912, he was elected the group's president. He also helped found the National Association for the Advancement of Colored People and served as a member of its board of directors and as a volunteer lawyer. Until his death in 1929 he was the foremost champion of Jewish rights in the United States.

Louis Marshall was considered the spokesperson for the American Jewish community from 1900 until his death in 1929. (American Jewish Historical Society)

Although a prominent leader of Reform Judaism, he said, "Nothing Jewish is alien to me" and was a founder of Conservative Judaism's Jewish Theological Seminary.

Between 1881 and 1914 close to two million Jews arrived in the United States from Russia, Poland, and Rumania—the impoverished countries of Eastern Europe. They were fleeing intolerable conditions with the hope of renewing their lives in the New World. Prior to this period, Jews and blacks in the United States had little daily contact with one another. Blacks, however, were deeply inspired by the biblical story of the Jewish Exodus from Egypt. Booker T. Washington wrote in *The Farthest Man Down,* "The most fascinating portion of the Bible was the story of the manner in which Moses led the children of Israel out of the house of bondage, through the wilderness, into the Promised Land.... The Negro slaves were always looking forward to a time when a Moses would arise from somewhere...."

Most blacks lived in the South: most of the newly arrived Jews settled in the urban centers of the North, many in New York City. But the Kishinev massacre struck a chord of sympathy in the black community and was condemned by African-American newspapers. They could not help remarking that among the signers of anti-Kishinev petitions were southern United States senators who supported the lynching of blacks.

The vast majority of Jewish-American immigrants had never seen a black person in Europe and knew little about their plight in the U.S. Once the new immigrants arrived, they were too busy concentrating on their own survival to even think about others. When a small group of new Jewish immigrants in New York took a stand against black voting rights in the South, Louis Marshall spoke up. "It seems incredible to me that a body of Jews who have just emerged from virtual slavery and who are seeking in this country the privilege of voting, which was withheld from them in the land in which their ancestors have lived, should for a moment consider the propriety of arguing in favor of the disfranchisement of any citizen of this country."

African-Americans and Jews eventually found themselves united in a common cause against discrimination. Both groups shared the status of "outsiders" in America and had to fight the stereotyped beliefs about them. The police commissioner of New York, pointing to the mass of impoverished immigrants, generalized publicly that Jewish teenagers in the Lower East Side were being "brought up to lives of crime." Newspaper headlines continued to identify black criminals by race, blaming an entire people for

Newly arrived Jewish immigrants crowded into New York's Lower East Side. (YIVO Institute for Jewish Research)

the actions of a few. Jews and blacks were outraged. They feared that all Americans would view them as promoters of criminal activity.

An 1893 article in *The New York Times* provides a glimpse of how Jewish immigrants were viewed by many Americans of the time. "This neighborhood [Lower East Side], peopled almost entirely by the people who claim to have been driven from Poland and Russia, is the eyesore of New York and perhaps the filthiest place on the eastern continent. It is impossible for a Christian to live there because he will be driven out either by blows or the dirt and stench. Cleanliness is an unknown quality to these people. They cannot be lifted up to a higher plane because they do not want to be." Strangely, the same descriptions were later applied to African-Americans living in the same urban ghettos, as if all poor people enjoyed being poor.

Although they should have been natural allies, it took two major events to bring Jews and blacks together. The first was the 1915 lynching of Leo Frank that shocked America. Not that lynchings were unknown in the country: hundreds of black men were brutally killed and tortured each year. What made this lynching a headline event was the fact that Leo Frank was a white man, and a Jew. Frank was the manager of the National Pencil Company plant in Atlanta, Georgia. In an atmosphere of anti-Semitism, Frank was sentenced to death, on extremely doubtful evidence, for sexually attacking and murdering a fourteen-year-old employee, Mary Phagan. The chief witness was a black janitor at the plant whose testimony was later discounted by a man who had worked in the company office and in 1982 revealed that he had seen the janitor with Mary Phagan's body. "The trial was the first time that a 'white' man was tried and convicted on the testimony of an African-American."

When all appeals had been exhausted, the governor of Georgia, doubting the evidence, commuted Frank's sentence to life imprisonment. On the night of August 16, 1915, an enraged mob stormed the prison, dragged Frank out, and lynched him. The young man's brutal murder "convinced many Jews of their vulnerability in the United States" and allied them with African-Americans in the struggle for universal civil rights.

The Anti-Defamation League of B'nai B'rith (ADL) was founded in 1913 as a result of the anti-Semitic reaction to the Frank case. The ADL was the idea of Sigmund Livingston, a Chicago attorney active in B'nai B'rith, "to protect the image of the Jew."

The second major event to bring Jews and blacks together was the Great Migration of African-Americans between 1915–1930. Prior to the outbreak of World War I, the vast majority of American blacks lived in the South. Spurred on by the economic chaos caused by floods and a blighted cotton crop, many African-Americans began to head North for new opportunities. New job openings in northern city factories lured more than one million blacks. Factories sent agents throughout the South to recruit skilled and unskilled workers for the steel mills and meatpacking houses. The black populations of New York City, Cleveland, Ohio; Gary, Indiana; Chicago, Illinois; and Philadelphia, Pennsylvania skyrocketed. One historian described the simultaneous migration by blacks and Jews to New York City as "refugees from the 'two

The lynching of Leo Frank, 1915. (American Jewish Archives)

Souths'—the Russian and the American—coming together on the banks of the Hudson."

The Jewish arrivals were quickly overwhelmed by the strange language and culture. Thousands of men, women, and children crowded into the squalid tenements and teeming streets of the Lower East Side. The only link between these poor, uneducated, "downtown" Jews and the successful, assimilated, second generation, "uptown" Jews was their shared religious and cultural heritage. It was that bond which brought the "uptowners" to the Lower East Side to aid the new arrivals. Foremost among them was a young Jewish nurse, Lillian Wald.

Lillian Wald was born in Cincinnati, Ohio, in 1867. She was trained as a nurse and had begun medical school when her life was changed by a series of visits to the Lower East Side of Manhattan. There, while teaching a course for immigrant women on home nursing, she realized that the impoverished families living in crowded tenements lacked basic health care. Instead of returning to medical school, she and another nurse, Mary Brewster, moved into a fifth-floor walk-up apartment on Henry Street. They began to offer nursing services to their neighbors to "contribute our sense of citizenship to what seems an alien group in a so-called democratic society."

With the help of wealthy "uptown" Jews, especially Jacob Schiff, Lillian Wald founded the Henry Street Settlement House in 1893. Schiff, born in Germany, was a financier and philanthropist. He was a strong supporter of the Jewish Theological Seminary and was especially concerned with bettering the lives of poor Jewish immigrants. The "Settlement" became the link between the German and Russian Jews as well as the African-American community. Wald always considered racial prejudice to be "the most absurd of bigotries." She was continuing a tradition begun by other established German Jews. As a member of the New York Board of Education, Jacob Schiff introduced a resolution calling for the "abolishment of separate schools of different races" on the grounds that they perpetuated "social and racial prejudice." German Jews also established the Free Kindergarten Association for Colored Children in 1895.

Nursing services alone could not solve the problems of the poor. Wald quickly realized that illness also had serious underlying social causes. She oversaw the

Lillian Wald. (Library of Congress)

establishment of integrated kindergartens, mothers' clubs, safe milk stations, and a variety of classes for adults and children. A summer camp for underprivileged children was one of the most popular activities.

The social work and nursing services instituted by Wald extended beyond the Lower East Side to other areas of the city. In 1906, she opened a branch of the Settlement in San Juan Hill, a predominantly African-American community in midtown Manhattan, west of Columbus Circle. By 1910, Wald and her nurses annually cared for over 15,000 patients, made over 140,000 home visits, and gave 18,000 first aid treatments. By 1925 one quarter of all the patients were black. "She was hardly conscious of sectarian or racial differences."

Lillian Wald was an active supporter of progressive causes. She fought hard on behalf of labor unions, women's voting rights, and world peace. In 1909 she was one of the signers of the call to establish the National Association for the Advancement of Colored People (NAACP). Her influence led Jacob Schiff, a contributor to Booker T. Washington's Tuskegee Institute, to also make financial gifts to the NAACP.

Wald and Schiff, like other Jewish supporters of civil rights, were responding to the basic teachings of Judaism as presented in the Bible.

On equality: "There shall be one law for you and for the resident stranger." (Numbers 15:16).

On freedom: "Proclaim liberty throughout the land to all the inhabitants thereof." (Leviticus 25:10).

The legendary leader of America's blacks at the turn of the century was Booker T. Washington. Born into slavery in 1856, he earned a teaching degree and ultimately founded the famed Tuskegee Institute. He deeply believed that blacks could elevate their condition through self-help, education in practical skills, material advancement, and home ownership. "Cast down your bucket where you are," he said, "cast it down in making friends in every manly way of the people of all races by whom we are surrounded." At the same time, he seemed to encourage segregation of the races. "In all things that are purely social," he wrote, "we can be as separate as the fingers. Yet one as the hand in things essential to mutual progress." He thought the future of black people rested in the South, where most of them lived. His philosophy appealed to many white philanthropists, including a number of prominent Jews, who contributed heavily to Tuskegee Institute. They believed that a gradual approach by blacks, emphasizing vocational training and home ownership, would eventually integrate African-Americans into the larger society. At the turn of the century, Jews constituted a majority of whites in attendance at Tuskegee commencement exercises. In his writings, Washington stated that African-Americans should model themselves on European Jews who as outcasts for nearly 2,000 years produced a world of their own within the larger world.

Although Washington was revered for pioneering work, other blacks thought him overly cautious and insensitive to the political and social realities of the time. William Edward Burghardt Du Bois was born in

Great Barrington, Massachusetts, in 1868. He graduated from Fisk University in Nashville, Tennessee, and became the first black to receive a doctorate from Harvard University. Later, he attended schools in Europe and returned to the United States with a view that differed from the teachings of Booker T. Washington. "In the history of nearly all other races and peoples," Du Bois wrote, "the doctrine preached has been that manly self-respect is worth more than lands and houses...." Arguing against Washington's views, Du Bois called for African-Americans to increase their political power, and strive for civil rights and higher education. Only by integrating into American society with full equality could blacks achieve respect. W. E. B. Du Bois proposed the development of the "Talented Tenth"—an elite of young, highly-educated, and talented blacks. "The Negro race, like all races, is going to be saved by its exceptional men," he wrote.

Years later, when asked about the place of Booker T. Washington in American history, Rabbi Stephen S. Wise responded: "It may be too early to attempt a final estimate of Mr. Washington's place in the history of our country and above all in the history of his race and its relation to the white world. I would say of Booker T. Washington that he was a great conciliator, that he did more than any man to bring his race to the understanding and sympathy of the white race and that, on the other hand, he made his own race more keenly understanding of the white race. This is his achievement."

Stephen S. Wise was born in Budapest, Hungary, in 1874. He arrived in America with his parents when he was very young. His father was a rabbi. After graduating from Columbia University in 1892, Stephen was ordained as a rabbi and began a long career that made him a towering figure in American religious and politi-

Rabbi Stephen S. Wise was at the forefront of progressive causes. He is shown with his son doing civilian work during World War I. (Library of Congress)

cal life. He spoke against political corruption, child labor, and injustice. He taught that Judaism was a caring and active religion. "For me," he said, "the supreme declaration of our Hebrew Bible was and remains 'Justice, justice shalt thou pursue' whether it be easy or hard, whether it be justice to white or black, Jew or Christian." Wise said his role as rabbi was "to plead for righteousness wherever and whenever unrighteousness obtains among men of earth and the things of earth." He taught that Judaism is a religion "which concerns itself with the affairs and doings of this life." Rabbi Wise was instrumental in founding the American Jewish Congress in 1918. Originally founded to combat anti-Semitism, it became particularly active in the civil rights struggles of the 1940s and 1950s.

Booker T. Washington's philosophy of nonconfrontational advancement was gradually weakened by increasing racial violence in the South and discrimination in the North. In July 1905, W. E. B. Du Bois gathered a group of thirty prominent black leaders at Fort Erie, Canada, just across the border at Niagara Falls. (Hotels on the American side would not admit them.) They founded the Niagara Movement dedicated to "aggressive action on the part of men who believe in Negro freedom and growth." Four years later, spurred on by violent race riots in Springfield, Illinois, Oswald Garrison Villard, grandson of a famed abolitionist, issued a "Call" for a conference "to discuss means for securing political and civil equality for the Negro." That "Call" was signed by three Jews: Lillian Wald, Rabbi Stephen S. Wise, and Dr. Henry Moskowitz, a New York activist social worker. The resulting meet-

Rabbi Stephen S. Wise. (Library of Congress)

ing drew upon the work of the Niagara Movement and years later led to the founding of the National Association for the Advancement of Colored People.

Rabbi Wise joined the NAACP "so as to cast in my lot with those determined to fight against injustice to Negroes." He was one of sixty Americans who signed the "Call," and was well-known for his vocal support of liberal causes. His "involvement with the NAACP probably resulted from his association with such independent progressives as Lillian Wald and Henry Moskowitz, who had been participating in regular meetings dealing with lynching and race-riots . . . " In the early years of the NAACP he served on the Advisory Committee and for the rest of his life always took an active role in fighting for equal rights for all. When asked in 1911 for his comments on prejudice, he said, "not only is race prejudice injurious to the welfare of a community, but it is an expression of lowered moral status and hence intensifies the ill-fare which begets it."

THE CALL TO ACTION

"Discrimination once permitted
cannot be bridled."

From "The Call"

The founding of the National Association for the Advancement of Colored People (NAACP) was a milestone in the struggle for civil rights. At a time when progressive voices were heard in the United States advocating for child labor laws, food safety, and women's right to vote, the NAACP stood alone in the fight against racism. "The objective of the NAACP in its formative period was to secure full citizenship and equal rights for the Negro through a militant but non-violent course of action." Its philosophy mirrored the activist thinking of Du Bois over the status-quo beliefs of Booker T. Washington.

Interestingly, one of the NAACP's first resolutions was a 1910 resolution condemning the violent pogroms against Jews in Russia. Seven Jews served on the first forty-five member General Committee including Lillian Wald, Rabbi Stephen S. Wise, Jacob Schiff, and Dr. Henry Moskowitz. Four Jews served on the first Executive Committee.

Lillian Wald remained an active member of the board until 1918 when other commitments required her attention. Her motto was "The whole world is my neighborhood." In 1914 she spoke before a meeting of the NAACP in New York about segregation. "Segregation discriminates against the individual without regard to proven worth or ability. No surer way could be found to injure the pride, the dignity and the self-respect of any person or people than to assume that, because of color, race, or nationality, they are unfit to mingle with the community." She urged people to work against newly initiated rules that segregated federal offices in Washington, D.C. "We commit ourselves to any wrong or degradation or injury when we do not protest against it," she said. After three years of inactive membership she resigned, insisting "it is not right to permit my name to continue in the organization when I am doing nothing and can attend no meetings."

Over the years other Jews took up positions on the board. William E. B. Du Bois, who in the early years was the NAACP's only black national officer, described the varied backgrounds of the white founders. "We had on our board of directors many incongruous elements as was to be expected: philanthropists like Oswald Villard; Social workers like Florence Kelley; liberal Christians like John Haynes Holmes and liberal Jews like the Spingarns; spiritual descendents of the Abolitionists like Mary Ovington and radical Negroes...."

Aside from the outspoken Du Bois, the name of Spingarn soon become synonymous with the NAACP. Joel E. Spingarn was born in New York in 1875 and his brother, Arthur, three years later. The independently wealthy Jewish brothers became prominent leaders of the NAACP. Joel Spingarn was a respected but controversial professor at Columbia University. He served as chairperson of the Department of Comparative Literature until a sharp disagreement with school administrators led to his dismissal. Freed from the routines and petty politics of academic life, Joel devoted the rest of his life to public service. His brother, Arthur, a well-known attorney, volunteered in 1913 to handle the growing legal work of the NAACP. For years, he served as the unpaid chairman of the NAACP's National Legal Committee.

Joel's interest in the fledgling NAACP arose when he read newspaper stories about Steve Greene, an African-American who had fled Arkansas for Chicago, Illinois, after accidentally killing his white landlord. The Arkansas sheriff who traveled to Chicago to return Greene told reporters that a lynch mob back home was prepared for Greene's homecoming. Moved by the brazen injustice, Spingarn said, "I don't care what happens, Steve Greene will never be extradited to Arkansas." He immediately sent Greene's defense fund a check for $100 and asked Greene's attorney for more

Arthur Spingarn, far right, served as the chairman of the NAACP's National Legal Committee for many years. (Schomberg Center for Research in Black Culture, New York Public Library)

information. Spingarn's interest in the case became known to NAACP leaders who immediately invited the well-known professor to serve on the association's executive committee. Spingarn's destiny and the future of the NAACP were permanently bonded.

The first goal of the NAACP was to free African-Americans unjustly accused of crimes, punish those responsible for lynchings, which Joel Spingarn described as a "stain on our civilization," and change the negative public image of black people. The NAACP preferred to do battle with discrimination in the courts, not on the streets.

Joel Spingarn held a number of positions with the NAACP. But his influence extended beyond titles. He served as chairperson of the NAACP Board of Directors from 1914–1919 and treasurer from 1919–1930. More importantly, he helped the new organization develop legal, political, and public relations strategies and became the public spokesperson for the NAACP. Joel Spingarn became president of the NAACP in 1929 and retained that position until 1939. When he died, Arthur assumed the presidency. In 1966, when Arthur retired from that position, Vice President Hubert Humphrey wrote him, "Your leadership in civil rights has spanned more than half a century in years but in terms of progress, it has spanned centuries."

In 1915 Joel established a prize to be awarded annually by the NAACP for "the highest and noblest achievement of an American Negro." His objective was to highlight the many contributions of African-Americans to science, literature, and politics and to demonstrate that talent was not limited to whites alone. Each year since, the awarding of the gold Spingarn Medal has been a major event in the African-American world. The first medal was given to Dr. Ernest Just of Howard University for his research in biology.

Like W. E. B. Du Bois, Joel Spingarn was opposed to Booker T. Washington's gradual approach. In a speech in Memphis, Tennessee, in 1914, Spingarn said, "It is possible that Dr. Washington is in a delicate position and cannot fight against Jim Crowism, segregation laws, and insulting intermarriage laws, but the friends of Dr. Washington certainly can and should join hands with those who stand with Du Bois in the battle against the erection of a monstrous caste system in this country."

Spingarn traveled the country organizing new NAACP chapters and speaking on what he called "The New Abolitionism." He urged blacks to join and prepare to eventually take over leadership roles in the organization from whites. "We white men of whatever creed or faith," he said, "cannot fight your battles for you. We will stand shoulder to shoulder with you until you can fight as generals all by yourselves." On another occasion he said, "I am tired of the philanthropy of rich white men toward your race. I want to see you fight your own battles with your own leaders and your own money."

Years later Spingarn wrote, "The real danger about race prejudice is not that it makes other people hate you, but that it may make you despise yourself. That was the danger I had chiefly in mind when I was touring the country.... I tried for that reason to rouse colored people rather than to convert white people."

Booker T. Washington died in 1915. The following year, Spingarn convened a meeting of all leaders of large black organizations at Troutbeck, his estate in Amenia, New York. Spingarn's goal was to obtain "resolutions supporting all forms of education for blacks—not just industrial arts." The leaders agreed to focus their activities on three major areas: the right to vote, equal education, and the end of racially-based violence.

The birth of the motion picture industry in the early part of the twentieth century gave rise to popular films which often depicted African-Americans and Jews as stereotypes. The Anti-Defamation League (ADL), founded in response to the anti-Jewish feelings generated by the Leo Frank case, fought against these stereotypical portrayals. The ADL declared that the "welfare of any one minority group in the United States is intertwined with the welfare of all, and that the welfare of all minorities is inseparable from the basic precepts of democracy." Since its creation, it has fought to secure fair treatment for all by vigorously opposing anti-Semitism and racism.

The 1915 release of the feature film *The Birth of a Nation* shocked America. Adapted from the best-selling novel *The Clansman*, the film portrayed the African-American as an "ignorant fool, a vicious rapist, a venal and unscrupulous politician or a faithful but doddering idiot," charged the NAACP magazine *Crisis*. A motion picture magazine said, "The Negroes are shown as horrible brutes, given over to beastly excesses, defiant and criminal in their attitude toward the whites and lusting after white women. Some of the details are plainly morbid and repulsive." Protests against the film from blacks and whites erupted throughout the country. Theater owners and film company executives were not silent either and mayors of major cities were caught in a political quandary. When the mayor of New York decided to permit the film to be shown, J. E. Spingarn sent a note to the NAACP secretary instructing her to "prepare as soon as possible a letter of protest to the Mayor against *The Birth of a Nation*, to be signed by Messrs. Villard, Spingarn, Du Bois, Holmes, Wise,

Schiff, Miss Wald...stating clearly the grounds of our objection."

In New York City, inspired by Lillian Wald, five hundred representatives of organizations supportive of African-American rights marched through the streets to a hearing at the mayor's office. Wald organized mass protests against the film after legal actions failed. The result was that some of the film's most objectionable scenes were deleted when it was shown in New York theaters. Joel Spingarn, Lillian Wald, and Jacob Schiff also protested to the National Board of Censorship of Motion Pictures, the group responsible for accrediting films for screening in theaters. At first the board agreed that the film should not be shown but the film's producers obtained court injunctions to prevent interference with further screenings.

Life for blacks in the South between 1890 and 1910 had become unbearable. Whatever rights African-Americans had gained during Reconstruction were systematically taken away. Black men, women, and children were constantly subject to indiscriminate violence. Between 1899 and 1916 the NAACP reported 3,244 cases of lynching of black men and women, mainly in the South. "The Shame of America" was the title of a leaflet issued by the NAACP in 1921 to educate the public about the continuing horror and to urge support of federal anti-lynching laws. "Do you know that the United States is the only land on Earth where human beings are burned at the stake?" the leaflet proclaimed. Lynching continued into the 1930s as the Ku Klux Klan boasted a national membership exceeding four million. Rabbi Stephen S. Wise was one of many

Jewish leaders who spoke out against the Klan. "The Klan could not be if we did not have in part...a false view of American and Americanism," he wrote. "America is not the possession of any man or any racial group or sectarian company, nor is it the possession of all of us....the citizenship of America belongs to it, and not America to its people."

Wise did not distinguish religion from activism for equal rights. Wise founded the Free Synagogue in New York explaining that "from the beginning, our plans with relation to social service as a part of the Synagogue life" was fundamental. Jacob Schiff, a Wise supporter, said, "The word of God heard in the Synagogue becomes of value only if it is carried into everyday life."

Time magazine reported in 1938 that "after 99.4 percent of U.S. lynchings [there were] no arrests, no indictments, no convictions." A 1933 editorial in a Tennessee newspaper decried the apparent involvement of law officials. "A mob is made up of cowards. Not many mobs will go through with a lynching without the active or tacit co-operation of the law officers who are paid to combat mobs."

Lynching may have been the most severe expression of racism; however, there were also lesser forms of discrimination. In 1910, residential segregation laws were instituted in Baltimore, Maryland. A year later, public transportation in southern states was segregated. Anti-intermarriage bills were introduced in northern legislatures. Violence against blacks continued to grow. In 1906, in Atlanta, Georgia, as many as fifty African-Americans were killed during five days of race rioting. Police were powerless to restrain the mobs that ruled the city. Quiet was not restored until the governor called out the National Guard. Riots against blacks also broke out in northern cities such as Akron, Ohio, and New York City.

Most American Jews, less than a generation removed from the pogroms of Eastern Europe, sympathized with the plight of African-Americans. The Yiddish language newspaper, the *Forward*, reported that "The situation of the Negroes in America is very similar to the situation of the Jews in Russia. The Negro diaspora, the special laws, the decrees, the pogroms and also the Negro complaints, the Negro hopes are very similar to those which we Jews experienced."

In a speech before the NAACP's annual meeting, Louis Marshall explained the reason for Jewish sympathy with the African-American struggle for equal rights: "I belong to an ancient race which has had even longer experience of oppression than you have. We came out of bondage nearly thirty centuries ago and we have had trouble ever since. In all parts of the world we have had to fight for our lives, for our existence, for our conscience.... We have been prevented in some countries from getting an education, from getting any opportunities of earning a livelihood.... We went from country to country. In Russia, in Poland ... we were subjected to indignities in comparison with which to sit in a "Jim Crow" car is to occupy a palace. Yet we have not given up and we are not going to give up."

Jewish sympathy for the plight of African-Americans went beyond the shared experiences of discrimination back to the fundamental teachings of Judaism: "Love your neighbor as yourself" (Leviticus 19:17–18),

"What is hateful to you, do not do unto your neighbor. This is the entire Torah: all the rest is commentary" (Talmud, Shabbat 8).

Despite the declining condition of African-Americans, advances were being made by the NAACP in the legal area. With the help of sympathetic lawyers, many of them Jewish, the wall of Jim Crow segregation began to crumble. Arthur Spingarn organized the legal battles for the NAACP. One of his first victories was the 1915 overturn of the infamous "grandfather clause," which exempted from strict state voting requirements those whose grandfathers had voted in 1867, thus keeping African-Americans from voting because their grandfathers had been slaves. The Yiddish language newspaper, the *Forward*, prematurely called the legal victory a "death blow to the Negro haters in the South."

Arthur Spingarn's legal advice ranged from Supreme Court cases to simple questions of copyright. No legal question was too minor if it held the hope of expanding equal rights to all citizens, and if the case had a good chance of succeeding in court. When, in 1929, an issue surfaced concerning the denial of service to African-American chauffeurs by garages, Arthur Spingarn analyzed the legal possibilities.

"The Civil Rights Act specifically mentions garages as places of public accommodation and therefore, any owner of a public garage who refuses accommodation to a colored man by reason of his color would be liable to the penalties provided by the statutes. There is however, a legal technicality... I do not think the question has ever come up, but the courts might hold that in the

79

case of a white owner having a colored chauffeur, the person aggrieved is not the colored chauffeur but the white owner. It is well to avoid such possible complications...it would be well to make the first test case one in which this point is not involved...."

Louis Marshall, considered the primary spokesperson of American Jews from 1900 until his death in 1929, volunteered his legal services to the NAACP. In one of his first appearances before the Supreme Court on behalf of the NAACP, he argued a case in which a white man in Washington, D.C., had attempted to sell his property to a black woman in contravention of a restrictive covenant which prohibited sale of the property "to any person of the negro race or blood." Basing his case on the Fourteenth Amendment guarantee of due process, requiring the government to treat all citizens with "fairness," Marshall argued in vain. "The moment that there is a differentiation in our courts between white and black, Catholic and Protestant, Jew and non-Jew," he said, "hatreds and passions will inevitably be aroused and that which has been most noble and exalted and humane in American life will have been shattered." Although Marshall died in 1929, his argument finally prevailed in 1948 when the Supreme Court outlawed restrictive covenants.

Prior to his appointment as the first Jewish member of the United States Supreme Court, Boston attorney Louis Brandeis helped plan the NAACP legal battle against Jim Crow railroad accommodations in the South. After Louis Marshall's death, another Jewish attorney, Felix Frankfurter, consulted on legal matters with the NAACP. Frankfurter also served as a member of the NAACP's National Legal Committee. He later followed Brandeis to a seat on the Supreme Court.

In 1911 another organization, the National Urban League (NUL), was founded by wealthy whites with support from Booker T. Washington. Its major objective was to assist African-Americans migrating to the northern big cities. While the NAACP focused on legal and public-relations methods, the NUL taught employment and living skills to African-American migrants to help them adjust to new lives in the cities. Unlike the NAACP, the founders of the NUL were black and white and included a number of Jews. Edwin R. A. Seligman, a professor of economics at Columbia University, was the organization's first chairperson. Lillian Wald served as a member of the Board of Directors. By 1920 one-third of the board was Jewish. "Many issues raised by black civil rights groups spoke directly to problems faced by American Jews—job discrimination, restrictive housing covenants, exclusion from universities and professions."

The NUL was more dependent upon contributions from wealthy donors than the NAACP. Between 1915 and 1919 nearly 40 percent of its operating budget came from three millionaires, John D. Rockefeller, Julius Rosenwald, and Alfred T. White. Both organizations received financial support from Jewish philanthropists and foundations.

When the United States entered World War I in 1917, the military was totally segregated. But in a spirit of patriotism, 700,000 black men registered for the draft and over 300,000 actually served overseas in segregated units. Joel Spingarn entered the army as an officer determined to secure officer training for capable African-American men. He offered to recruit black university students for officer training and to buy uniforms for them. He knew that black officers could only command black troops, but any objection to that racist tradition might be seen by whites as unpatriotic. "I do not believe," Spingarn said, "that colored men should be separated from other Americans in any field of life but that the crisis was too near to debate principles and opinions."

Spingarn successfully fought opposition to his plan that arose within the NAACP. Many black leaders wanted nothing less than complete integration of the troops. A segregated army was demeaning to blacks and sent a clear message that African-Americans were less than equal citizens. Spingarn sympathized with that argument but wrote, "It seems to me that there is only one thing for you to do at this juncture and that is to get the training that will fit you to be officers, however and wherever and whenever this training may be obtained." Spingarn pressed on and the NAACP ultimately backed his plan. By the end of the war over six hundred blacks were commissioned as officers in the United States Army. More importantly, they had received valuable training which would carry over into civilian life.

The Great Migration of blacks to northern cities continued unabated during World War I. The job market boomed as factories worked day and night to fill military orders. Although the Jewish president of the American Federation of Labor, Samuel Gompers, promised to remove "every class and race distinction" from the national labor movement, only two predominantly Jewish unions voted to admit blacks to equal membership—the International Ladies Garment Workers Union (ILGWU) and the Amalgamated Clothing Workers.

By the 1930s blacks began taking over leadership roles from whites in the NAACP. While Jews continued to serve as chairman, president, and head of the Legal Committee, day-to-day operations were carried out by a growing number of black professionals. Indeed, the election of J. E. Spingarn as NAACP president in 1929 created a stir in the African-American community. "Negroes Divided on White Leader," one newspaper headlined. "The controversy over whether Negroes are to lead their own campaign for advancement as a race, or select outstanding white men as leaders has broken out afresh...."

Spingarn, who served as president until his death in 1939, understood the dissent and realized that positive changes in race relations were a natural outcome of joint efforts by whites and blacks. Years earlier, in 1921, he had written about the growing self-pride of African-Americans. "A new sense of their power and destiny is in the very soul of black men and women.... in the end it will force both races to seek and find some form of compromise or adjustment by which they can live peacefully and with self-respect together."

HELPING PEOPLE
HELP THEMSELVES

"Freedom, my friends, does not come from
the clouds...it does not come without great
efforts and great sacrifices: all who love
liberty have to labor for it."

Ernestine Rose

Julius Rosenwald was born on August 12, 1862, in
Springfield, Illinois, to Jewish parents who immigrated
to the United States from Germany. Leaving school at
age seventeen, he headed to New York where he
worked in a cousin's store selling men's clothing. Six
years later, he returned to Illinois where he opened his
own men's clothing store in Chicago. He had good
business sense, and soon befriended two young men,
Richard Sears and Alvah Roebuck, who were not

doing too well starting up a revolutionary mail order business. When Alvah Roebuck wanted to sell his share of the firm to Richard Sears, Sears raised the money by offering half the business to Rosenwald and a Rosenwald cousin. Rosenwald invested $37,500 in what soon turned out to be a most profitable business venture. By 1909, Sears had retired and Rosenwald was president of a firm with over 10,000, employees and a catalog as widely read in the United States as the Bible.

A modest man, he was soon perplexed by the amount of money he was earning. "I really feel ashamed to have so much money," he once remarked. He decided early to put his money to good use and once told a friend his goal was to set aside one-third of his income for charitable purposes. Rosenwald practiced the Jewish concept of charity known as "tzedakah," from the Hebrew word for "just," which is integral to the Jewish way of life.

Rosenwald was largely responsible for organizing the Jewish Charities of Chicago, which he served as president. He later became national vice president of the American Jewish Committee and an officer of his Chicago synagogue, Sinai Congregation. One of his favorite Jewish charities in Chicago was the Jewish Home Finding Association, which placed orphan children in private homes rather than orphanages.

From the beginning, he was a strong supporter of black philanthropy, especially interested in helping the NAACP combat lynching and providing legal services. He was inspired by the writings of Booker T. Washington and soon became one of Tuskegee Institute's prime

Julius Rosenwald and his wife. (Library of Congress)

supporters. In a January 9, 1920, letter to the NAACP, Rosenwald's secretary wrote, "Mr. Rosenwald is in sympathy with the plan of the National Association for the Advancement of Colored People to aid the Arkansas riot-convicted Negroes in carrying their cases up on appeal.... To help this cause, it will give Mr. Rosenwald pleasure to add $500 to each $4500 collected, up to a total of $25,000."

"It is easier for a man to make $1,000,000 honestly," Rosenwald said, "than to dispose of it wisely." His first major philanthropic contribution was not to a Jewish charity but to the YMCA, the Young Men's Christian Association. When the Chicago YMCA approached him about a contribution for a new building fund, Rosenwald inquired whether a building was planned for African-American men. When told that no such building was planned, Rosenwald responded that he would be happy to donate $25,000 whenever the YMCA was ready for such a project. It did not take long before a new YMCA building for blacks was built in Chicago.

In 1910 Rosenwald made an offer to the national YMCA. He promised to donate an additional $25,000 to any city which raised $75,000 to build a YMCA for African-Americans. He strongly believed that local people needed to participate in all charitable undertakings. Within a ten-year period, twenty-four well-equipped YMCA buildings rose to serve black communities in such cities as Washington, New York, Philadelphia, Atlanta, Los Angeles, and Buffalo. Most of the Rosenwald YMCAs were located in or near black business districts. By the mid-1930s there were 20,000 registered members and many thousands more who took advantage of the YMCA programs. There is no doubt that these buildings provided educational and recreational programs that improved the lives of many.

At the dedication of the Chicago YMCA he helped build, Rosenwald told those in attendance, "You now have an enterprise in which you have participated from the start, for you conducted a campaign for raising money.... you are organizing the force to operate the plant. You are going to run it, too. . . . What a grand opportunity to grow strong! What an efficient help to dissipate prejudice!"

While it is true that Rosenwald did not encourage the integration of YMCA facilities, he strongly supported the separate but equal philosophy espoused in the Plessy v. Ferguson case and the teachings of Booker T. Washington. His goal was not to provide charity but opportunities for black self-help and personal development. He hoped to induce blacks and whites to work together and to provide African-Africans "an opportunity, not to be worked *for* but to be worked *with*."

Booker T. Washington called Rosenwald's YMCA program "one of the wisest and best-paying philanthropic investments." In turn, Rosenwald credited Washington with directing the philanthropist's interests in the black community. After reading Washington's autobiography, *Up From Slavery,* Rosenwald invited Washington, the president of Tuskegee Institute, to speak at a Chicago business meeting in 1911. In his introduction, the Sears, Roebuck president said, "Whether it is because I belong to a people who have known centuries of persecution or whether it is because naturally I am inclined to sympathize with the oppressed, I have always felt keenly for the colored race."

Five months later he organized the first of several private railroad car trips of friends and relatives to Tuskegee Institute to introduce the work of Booker T. Washington to others. A primary concern was the state of education of young African-Americans in the South. In honor of his fiftieth birthday in 1912, Julius Rosenwald made a sizable contribution to Tuskegee

Institute. Booker T. Washington asked if a portion of the money might be used to build several elementary schools for blacks nearby. Rosenwald agreed but with the same stipulation he had attached to his YMCA contributions. Each community had to raise enough money to match his gift. This experiment led to the establishment of the Rosenwald Schools.

Out of his trips to Tuskegee and the success of the YMCA model of cooperation emerged a plan to help African-Americans in the South raise the quality of education. After the Civil War, the federal government urged southern states to provide public education for both white children and the children of freed slaves. By the turn of the century, worsening economic conditions and inattention to the separate but equal interpretation of Plessy v. Ferguson led to increased differences in quality between white and black schools.

At the end of the Civil War, northern churches and other groups had contributed funds toward black education in the South. Most of that money was earmarked for the training of teachers. That training was not enough to surmount the reality of dilapidated school buildings, lack of sufficient school supplies, and meaningful supervision.

Rosenwald hired investigators who studied one Alabama county's schools. They found that in white schools there were thirty students to one teacher while in the black community one teacher was responsible for over two hundred students. The county spent $14 for the education of each white child and only twenty cents for each black child. A majority of blacks who lived in the South had little chance of receiving any meaningful education.

Rosenwald was shocked. He built six schools in the county, predicated on the financial participation of local governments. The experiment was so successful that Rosenwald expanded his role in school-building in the South. The first Rosenwald School opened in Alabama in 1913. Within two years the Sears, Roebuck president had given money for the establishment of eighty more schools. Rosenwald insisted that each school "had to represent common effort by the state and county authorities and local colored and white citizens. The state and county had to contribute to the building and agree to maintain it as a regular part of the public school system." In October, 1917, he chartered the Julius Rosenwald Fund, which remained under his direct control until 1928 when he turned responsibilities over to a board of directors. The amazing stipulation was that the fund had to spend all its money within twenty-five years of Rosenwald's death.

The fund is credited with the building of 5,295 schools for black children in fifteen southern states. As was Rosenwald's philosophy from the beginning, no grants were outright. Each amount of Rosenwald Fund money had to be matched by the receiving community. The purpose was to make local and state governments responsible for future maintenance of their black schools.

Rosenwald Fund officials prepared detailed construction blueprints for a variety of schools. Included were floor plans for specific size schools which included residences for teachers, paint color for the buildings, and landscaping details. Assistance was provided to local communities in every aspect of the project from fund-raising to school-desk placement. The fund-raising became a community-wide lesson in cooperation. A flyer announcing a "Financial Educational Rally" in 1929 invited local African-Americans to join with their neighbors in hearing from "prominent visitors." Those not quite convinced were enticed by the words "Free dinner served." The seriousness of the event was impressed on everyone. "Realizing the fact that the only medium through which any race can achieve success is by its people, we are inviting every community, school and church to be present in order that our goal might be successfully reached."

Each year, Rosenwald Day exercises were held in the community schools to "re-arouse community interest in schools, encourage the cleaning and beautifying of the school buildings and grounds and to raise money for needed repairs or additions to equipment."

The Rosenwald schools were a vast improvement over what had previously passed for schools. Old, tumble-down buildings gave way to modern-looking schoolhouses with large windows. Most schools for whites and blacks offered education only through the eighth grade and students in rural areas rarely went on to high school. The future was even more limited for African-American children. One former black Rosenwald student recalled, "Where we was going, there wasn't much hope. The only thing a black person could do then was teach a little bit in a black school."

When Julius Rosenwald died in 1932, his philanthropic activity was praised for making a difference in
people's lives. He was called "one of the greatest
friends of the Negro race since Abraham Lincoln." At a
memorial service, the rabbi of his congregation said,
"Rosenwald's devotion to the cause of uplifting the
Negro was...one of the most intensely Jewish things
that Rosenwald ever did." With his death, the fund
curtailed the school building program to prevent communities from becoming reliant on outside aid. The
fund, however, continued its mission of upgrading educational opportunities for young blacks.

While the Rosenwald Schools made a difference
in the lives of many southern African-Americans in
the 1920s and 1930s, the illiteracy rate remained
high and only one-half of school-age children, white
and black, attended classes. One statistic showed
that in 1930 there were only 60,000 high school graduates in the South. As black families continued their
migration to northern cities, the Rosenwald Fund
shifted its grants to improve library services and
teacher-training institutions. Fund officials were concerned with the ineffective training of black teachers and unavailability of quality educational
materials for students.

Health education opportunities created by the
Rosenwald Fund included schools for nurses and support for community health clinics. Four quality black
universities were also supported with Rosenwald
funds, including famed Howard University in Washington, D.C., founded in 1867 through the Freedmen's
Bureau; Atlanta University in Georgia; Fisk University

in Nashville, Tennessee; and Dillard University in New Orleans, Louisiana.

Over a twenty-year period the fund awarded fellowships to promising young southern blacks and whites to study at northern universities. The one thousand black and five hundred white recipients became the community leaders of the next generation. Toward the end of its existence in the 1930s and 1940s, leaders of the fund also began using its influence to end race segregation in education, the federal government, churches, and the military.

True to Julius Rosenwald's word, the fund put itself out of business in 1948. It was the "most influential philanthropic force that came to the aid of Negroes at that time. Rosenwald understood that social conditions change." The work of the fund succeeded in raising the level of state support for black students and for many was the only link to a decent elementary education. In 1948, there was still a lot more to be done, but means other than direct philanthropy would have to be used.

One of the thousands of Rosenwald Fund beneficiaries was the African-American artist, Jacob Lawrence. Son of parents who took part in the Great Migration, Lawrence created his famous cycle of sixty paintings which captured the mood of the Great Migration. He himself had been born in Atlantic City, New Jersey, in 1917 to parents who were on that northern-bound journey. His "Migration Series," begun in 1940, vividly chronicles the emotions of the nearly one million African-American men, women, and children who left their homes in the South to seek better lives in the North. Today, the "Migration

Series" paintings are housed at the Museum of Modern Art in New York and the Phillips Collection in Washington, D.C.

Edwin Rogers Embree, who served as president of the fund from 1928 to 1948, said, "The Negro does not receive educational opportunity equal to white students of the same community in any separate school system.... Equality of educational opportunity will be fully realized only when segregation is outlawed." But it remained for the legal activities of the NAACP to finally break down the barriers of segregation that prevented equal education for all children in the United States. It was not an easy struggle.

By the turn of the century, despite the efforts of supporters like Rosenwald, the lofty ideals of Booker T. Washington had been subverted. Even the "separate but equal" philosophy represented in Plessy v. Ferguson could not withstand the white extremism that overtook the South. A way of life had entrenched itself in the guise of discriminatory laws which placed African-Americans in the position of inferior citizens, with few rights and even fewer opportunities. The governor of Mississippi bluntly warned, "if it is necessary, every Negro in the state will be lynched: it will be done to maintain white supremacy."

Discrimination in the United States was neither limited to the South nor to African-Americans. Immigrants, in general, and Jews, in particular, were frequent targets. In the 1920s major universities established quotas limiting the number of Jewish students. The president of Harvard University explained that "the anti-Semitic feeling among students is increasing, and it grows in proportion to the increase in...Jews." Harvard also banned its few African-American students from university dormitories. "We have not thought it possible," the president said, "to compel men of different races to live together."

Discrimination against Jews and African-Americans in housing and accommodations was even more blunt. "No Negroes Admitted Here," "Hebrew patronage not requested." Leaflets were often distributed to homeowners urging them not to sell property to Jews or Negroes. When Louis Marshall represented the NAACP in overturning a housing restriction against

Juden und Kinder.

Anti-Semites in Europe portrayed Jews as evil and devious. This scene from a German children's picture book from the 1920s was typical. (Library of Congress)

Washington, D.C., blacks, he did so "in the hope that it may incidentally benefit Jews."

Henry Ford, the great American industrialist, led a campaign against Jews. In his newspaper, the *Dearborn Independent*, he blamed Jews for the world's problems. Organizations such as the American Jewish Committee and the American Jewish Congress fought back. When Ford finally discontinued his attacks on Jews, Julius Rosenwald issued a statement to a Chicago newspaper. "...it is never too late to make amends and I congratulate Mr. Ford that he has at last seen the light. He will find that the spirit of forgiveness is not entirely a Christian virtue, but is equally a Jewish virtue."

The work of Marshall, Rosenwald, Washington, and the organizations they represented was, for the most part, accomplished through quiet negotiation, not loud, public agitation. Jewish-Americans and African-Americans, until the end of the Second World War, feared being thought of as "too pushy" by society at large. Later, Jews called this the "sha sha syndrome"— from the Yiddish expression for "be quiet;" don't make waves and you won't attract attention from those who dislike you.

Jews did not remain quiet all the time. Politicians soon realized the importance of Jewish voters who took seriously their right to vote. In 1913, after years of political lobbying, the state of New York passed a civil rights bill that prohibited discrimination in advertising, hotels, and theaters.

Adapting to an urban lifestyle was difficult. Like the European immigrants who crowded into their own city ghettos, African-Americans, by their sheer numbers, soon claimed large sections of major cities. Although more work opportunities were open to them, their lives, in many ways, were likely to be just as segregated in the North as they were in the South. Like the European immigrants, they were not prepared for urban living. Local Urban Leagues taught newcomers about city ways, urging them to avoid "loud talking and objectionable deportment on street cars and in public places" and to "refrain from wearing dust caps, bungalow aprons, house clothing and bedroom shoes out of doors."

One of the first white groups the newly arrived blacks met in the North were the Jews. Most in each group had never previously met anyone from the other group. The newcomers often settled in the same sections of large cities where Jews had begun to arrive a generation earlier. Aside from sharing the same goals and real estate, there were major differences between the groups. The African-Americans came to the big cities with farming experiences not useful in a Detroit factory, for example. The majority of Jews who came from Russia and were not allowed to own land in the "Old Country" were shopkeepers or tradespeople who continued in those vocations when they arrived in America. As the Jews advanced economically, they began to move to the suburbs. Some with established businesses in the urban neighborhoods remained behind to serve new black clientele. Unfortunately, the familiarity did not always produce positive reactions.

7

THROUGH LEGAL MEANS

"Civil rights is not a Negro cause:
it is a human cause."

Jack Greenberg

Discrimination knows no boundaries. Although African-Americans were at a greater disadvantage in the 1920s and 1930s, Jews also felt the stings of hatred and bias: sometimes in similar ways and sometimes differently. African-Americans who had migrated North with hope during World War I saw their dreams shattered. Even as the migration continued, jobs reverted to returning white soldiers. Black hopes were quickly replaced by disease, crime, and poverty. Conditions were even worse for the vast majority of African-Americans who remained in the South. Jim Crow laws in the South and institutional racism in the

North ordained blacks to a state of subservience in a white world.

In a blunt address to returning World War I black soldiers, W. E. B. Du Bois said, "We stand again to look America squarely in the face. It lynches...it disfranchises...it insults us...we return fighting. Make way for Democracy! We saved it in France, and by the great Jehovah, we will save it in the U.S.A." It would take more than rhetoric to make his words come true.

Jews also faced continuing discrimination. Strict quotas in the "Old Country" had limited the number of Jews admitted to high schools and universities and strict discriminatory rules determined where they could live and what professions they could enter. When they arrived in the United States at the turn of the century, they settled in urban areas and engaged in such occupations as tailoring, carpentry, jewelry, and hat making. Children of these immigrants moved out of their parent's ghettos as quickly as they could. Most escaped from the ghetto by conventional hard work. They went to school, obeyed laws, and became mainstream Americans. Many took advantage of public education and gained admission to universities to study law, accounting, and medicine. Others held jobs in factories or expanded family businesses: pushcarts were transformed into successful stores. Yet, as they began the move from the Jewish ghettos, Jews, like blacks, began to experience intensive discrimination and prejudice but in different ways.

Jews were charged with controlling American business even though they were systematically excluded from management positions in such important fields as

Interior of a "sweatshop." (YIVO Institute for Jewish Research)

banking, insurance, and public utilities. They were largely confined to small businesses and those larger industries that they helped create, including films, broadcasting, and retailing. Discrimination continued against Jews in private clubs, resorts, and private schools. As early as 1913, the American Jewish Committee successfully persuaded the New York state legislature to pass a bill forbidding places of public accommodation from advertising any admission restrictions because of race, creed, or color. Nonetheless, Jews were still barred from many resorts and clubs.

Anti-Semitism continued largely unabated. A small but highly visible minority of immigrant children achieved success in less conventional ways by pursuing show business or criminal careers. These children of immigrants were less bound by Old World traditions than their parents. Most were born into lives of poverty and were quickly influenced by the behavior of the streets. No single group of ghetto graduates gave more pride to their immigrant parents and neighbors than the popular singers, actors, and comedians such as Eddie Cantor, Sophie Tucker, and George Burns. No group provided more embarrassment than the gangsters such as "Bugsy" Siegel and "Dutch" Schultz. Their exploits (and killings) were avidly followed by millions in the daily newspapers.

Jews, like blacks, found themselves tarnished as a group for the exploits of a few. When New York's police commissioner wrote a 1908 magazine article on crime in his city, he singled out the Jews for special mention. "They are burglars, firebugs, pickpockets, and highway robbers," he declared and then added that "among the most expert of all the street thieves are Hebrew boys under sixteen who are brought up to lives of crime." In spite of a significant Jewish presence in the entertainment world—most Hollywood movie studios were owned by Jews—the police commissioner's thoughts continued to be reflected in plays and movies that depicted Jews as criminals. "It must have appeared," one historian later wrote, "as though the Jews had a monopoly on American crime."

No American was more famous in the 1920s than Henry Ford. His production ideas made the automobile an American obsession. He was equally influential in

Working conditions in "sweatshops" affected the health of workers. (Archives of Labor and Urban Affairs, Wayne State University)

spreading anti-Semitic ideas across America. Beginning in 1920, Ford's newspaper, the *Dearborn Independent,* embarked on an anti-Semitic crusade against the "international Jew." Week after week, the newspaper accused Jews of dominating American politics and economics. As major "proof" Ford reprinted the *Protocols of the Elders of Zion,* a forgery written several years earlier by Russian secret police to discredit Jews. The *Protocols* described, in specific but imaginative detail, an international Jewish conspiracy to control the world.

Ford's charges against Jews had a receptive audience in America. The period following World War I was a time of uncertainty. A fear of communism followed the Russian Revolution of 1917 and led to the rise of emotional patriotism and suspicion of minorities and strangers. The 1924 Immigration Act literally closed the door to immigrants. Jews, blacks, and Asians were particularly affected. It was also a time of growth for the Ku Klux Klan, which escalated a terror campaign against African-Americans.

While the NAACP continued its public anti-lynching campaign, American Jewish organizations tried to battle discrimination in their own more private ways. The American Jewish Committee, whose elite membership preferred soft-spoken individual discussions rather than the spectacle of public demonstrations, debated the idea of sponsoring academic studies on prejudice. One committee leader, Cyrus Sulzberger, publisher of *The New York Times,* believed that all the debate merely delayed implementation of workable solutions. He feared that "almost any day we may find conditions here much worse than they have been in the past." He was right.

Adolph Hitler came to power in Germany in 1933. After years of threats against Jews, the Nazis were now in a position to carry them out. Rabbi Stephen S. Wise, then the Honorary President of the American Jewish Congress, wrote, "I cannot remember Jewry being so wrought up against anything happening to American Jews as the sudden reversion on the part of a great and cultured and liberty-loving people [Germany] to practices which may be mildly characterized as medieval."

At home, America First and other so-called patriotic groups kept the fires of anti-Semitism burning. The American Jewish Congress sadly commented, "At no time in American history has anti-Semitism been as strong as it is today. At no time has that particularly smug, mealy-mouthed, 'some of my best friends are Jews' type of anti-Semitism received such widespread public utterance on political platforms, in the houses of Congress and in the news."

Strict immigration laws kept many German Jews from safety in the United States. But even American Jewish leaders, nervous about raising public debate about a Jewish issue, did not realize just how threatened were the lives of European Jews. Testifying at a congressional hearing on seeking a one-time relaxation of strict rules to admit 20,000 refugee children, Rabbi Wise said, "I want to make it plain that, so far as I am concerned there is no intention whatsoever to depart from the immigration laws which at present obtain..." Not as shyly, the Jewish Labor Committee bluntly said, "America must not lock her doors in the face of

105

these helpless, these suffering men and women."
In spite of the country's unwillingness to face world
realities, a new president began to assert his authority
on domestic matters.

When Franklin Delano Roosevelt was first elected
president in 1932, it was with little black support. He
was, after all, a Democrat and it was the Republican
Party of Abraham Lincoln that had supported the emancipation of the slaves. But the country was in the midst
of the Great Depression and no group in America was
suffering more than African-Americans. Roosevelt's pop-
ularity among blacks grew as federal programs were
introduced by the new administration to combat the
overwhelming poverty. The open advocacy of civil rights
by his wife, Eleanor, also added to the president's stature.
Roosevelt's New Deal was welcomed by African-Americans. Nearly one-quarter of all city-dwelling blacks
received public assistance; jobs were nearly impossible
to obtain and half of all blacks were unemployed. In the
1936 presidential election, Roosevelt received the overwhelming majority of black votes cast.

During his presidency, Roosevelt appointed a number of African-American lawyers, educators, and econ-
omists to high government positions. This was a first.
Washington, D.C., was itself segregated: African-
Americans might be able to work for the government
but they had to eat in separate restaurants and sit apart
from whites in theaters and on buses.

One event of the 1930s clearly defines the division
between blacks and whites. Marion Anderson, one of the
most famous opera stars of the time, also happened to be
an African-American. Because of discrimination at

home, she traveled to Europe in 1934 on a Rosenwald Fund scholarship. There, the American concert agent Sol Hurok, a Jew, discovered her and urged her to return home. Back in the United States Hurok managed Anderson's concert tours. In 1938, Howard University requested a performance by Marion Anderson in Washington, D.C. Hurok set a date and routinely contacted the Daughters of the American Revolution (DAR) for use of their Constitution Hall. Hurok was denied use of the hall for Ms. Anderson since a clause in the lease prohibited blacks from performing there. Hurok was angry. He contacted the press, and the news electrified the world. Eleanor Roosevelt resigned from the DAR.

Hurok took advantage of the adverse public opinion and arranged a unique outdoor concert for Ms. Anderson on Easter Sunday, 1939, at the Lincoln Memorial. In a superb concert broadcast live across the nation, Ms. Anderson sang brilliantly to a crowd of 75,000 that included members of Congress and the Supreme Court. "When I stood up to sing our national anthem," she later recounted, "I felt for a moment as though I were choking. For a desperate second I thought that the words would not come."

While the NAACP continued to fight in the courts for the removal of all signs of discrimination, Jewish attention was focused on Germany and the growing peril to Europe's Jews. Not wishing to call undue attention to itself, the Jewish community was largely silent, invoking the "Sha! Sha! Syndrome." Sha!—keep quiet and out of the limelight so your enemies won't have a target to attack. For many Jews, their religion had become a source of anxiety and discomfort. The *B'nai B'rith Mag-*

azine described the effect in the 1936 election campaign: "During the election campaign just over we heard a great deal to this effect: that the Jew efface himself as much as possible from public life lest he appear too prominent and make himself a shining mark for enemies."

There was no lack of enemies. One of the most prominent in the late 1930s was a Roman Catholic priest, Father Charles Coughlin. Father Coughlin discovered the power of radio to broadcast a political agenda to a nationwide audience. He began as a religious broadcaster but soon turned to right-wing political causes and religious intolerance, particularly against Jews. Prior to the outbreak of World War II, his program was one of the most popular on radio.

Father Coughlin revived the long-discredited *Protocols of the Elders of Zion*, telling listeners, "I emphasize once more that I am not interested in the authenticity of the Protocols. I am interested in their factuality." He promoted the views of America First, opposed United States involvement in the coming world war, and justified Nazism as a "defense reaction" against Jewish power. Another famous America Firster was aviator Charles A. Lindbergh, the first person to fly across the Atlantic. His hero status was tarnished in the minds of many by his isolationist, anti-Semitic, and pro-German remarks prior to World War II. In response to the America Firsters, Rabbi Stephen Wise stated, "We are Americans first, last and all the time. Nothing else that we are, whether by faith or race or fate, qualifies our Americanism."

In 1925, at a time when most labor unions excluded African-Americans, A. Philip Randolph organized the

Brotherhood of Sleeping Car Porters. Over the years, his union was one of the most active in gaining rights and benefits for its exclusively African-American membership. Randolph was born in 1899 in Florida. As a young man he moved North where he attended the

Jews as well as blacks were constantly reminded that bigotry was alive in the United States. (YIVO Institute for Jewish Research)

City College of New York. He worked as a porter and waiter and began to realize that only low paying jobs were available to African-Americans like himself. He devoted the rest of his life to empowering black workers through organized labor.

A handful of other unions, notably the International Ladies Garment Workers, with its predominantly Jewish leadership, were also at the forefront. In 1934, the ILGWU formed a special "Negro Department" under the control of a full-time black organizer. The following year, as meat prices in New York butcher shops rose dramatically, Jewish and African-American women organized by the labor unions jointly picketed neighborhood butcher shops. Eventually they forced the closing of nearly 4,500 shops throughout New York until meat prices were lowered.

In 1941, the NAACP held protest meetings in twenty-six states demanding equal apportionment of jobs for blacks. The defense industry, responding to the demands of World War II, was operating at near capacity and people were needed to fill the new job openings. The response from many large firms was disappointing. "We haven't had a Negro worker in twenty-five years and do not plan to start now," was a typical comment from one plant manager. Another responded, "It is against company policy to employ Negroes as aircraft workers and mechanics. There will be some jobs as janitors."

Something dramatic was needed to convince President Roosevelt that the time had come for equal employment opportunities for blacks. The First World War had not offered African-Americans a lasting opportunity for meaningful employment. In 1941, with the Second World War already underway in Europe, and American participation expected momentarily, blacks

אידיש. — יא, עם קלינגט אונגלויבליך, אבער ס'איז א פאקט. אז דער מאן, וועלכען מ'זעֶר
לערענט זיך די אידישע שפראך. דער וועלטענער אידיש-לערנער הייסט מיישאק ניל א
פון דער דרעס-פרעסערס יוניאן, לאקאל 60, אין ניו יארק. ניל באזוכט די אידישע קורסֿ
ערנעשאנעל לאקאל האט לעצטענס אייגעפֿיהרט. רעכטס זיצט רעימאנד געבינער, ד;
יי קורסען. ער איז דער עדיוקעישאנעל דירעקטאר פון לאקאל 60. דוישעק ספיטצער א
דער מישטרמאז פז בילדונגס-מאמיטעט פון דעם לאמאל.

An African-American member of a mostly Jewish clothing union learns Yiddish to better communicate with his Jewish co-workers. Clothing unions like the ILGWU were first to welcome African-American members. (YIVO Institute for Jewish Research)

111

were not about to accept a replay. Simple protest meetings were not achieving results.

A. Philip Randolph had an idea—a march on Washington. "The administration leaders," Randolph said, "will never give the Negro justice until they see ten, twenty, fifty thousand Negroes on the White House lawn." To the surprise of sympathetic whites, Randolph politely said, "We shall not call upon our white friends to march with us. . . . there are some things Negroes must do alone." Enthusiastic people responded to Randolph's "Call to Negro America" and signed up to be in Washington on July 1, 1941. Hundreds of buses were chartered and more were sought to accommodate the growing number of people. President Roosevelt became concerned. The last thing he wanted to see was a huge protest on his front lawn at a time when national unity was required.

Roosevelt invited Randolph and NAACP President Walter White to the White House on June 18. "What do you want me to do?" he asked them. "Issue an executive order abolishing discrimination in all government departments and national defense jobs," Randolph replied. On June 25, 1941, President Roosevelt issued Executive Order 8802. "There shall be no discrimination," read the order, "in the employment of workers in defense industries or government because of race, creed, color or national origin." In addition, Roosevelt created the Fair Employment Practices Commission (FEPC) to oversee compliance with the order. The march was canceled. Randolph had won. The following year, the NAACP presented its coveted Spingarn Medal to A. Philip Randolph. By the end of the war there were six times as many black union members as in 1940.

More than one million African-Americans served in the armed forces of the United States during World War II, mostly in segregated support units behind the front lines. Like most of American society, the army operated according to Jim Crow rules, particularly at southern military bases. Even Red Cross blood supplies were segregated. When, in 1942, black newspapers attacked these policies, the government threatened to charge them with sedition. There were, however, some high points. In 1940, Benjamin O. Davis became the first African-American general in the United States Army. After much pressure, the War Department organized a flight school for black pilots at Tuskegee, Alabama. The fighting record of the Tuskegee Airmen was impressive: eighty-two graduates received the Distinguished Flying Cross for bravery and success under fire.

In 1944 the War Department issued orders forbidding discrimination at off-duty activities at all military bases. Although the orders were largely ignored on the local level, they marked a shift in official government attitude. As Walter White of the NAACP visited with black troops overseas, he told them, "Our battle for democracy will begin when we reach home."

Even before the war ended, an active alliance against prejudice was taking shape in the United States. When news of the Holocaust began filtering through the Nazi-imposed curtain of secrecy, the NAACP passed a formal resolution in support of Jews. The NAACP pledged "its unqualified and unlimited effort on behalf of the persecuted Jews in the world, which includes anti-Semitism in the United States as well as mass slaughter in Poland."

The wall of self-created anonymity Jews defensively threw around themselves began to crumble. The Holocaust shocked Jewish Americans into the realization that they had to actively combat hatred, discrimination, and prejudice at home. When the war ended, Jews had become the most "racially liberal of all white groups." They began by strengthening their own existing "defense" organizations. The leadership of the Anti-Defamation League, American Jewish Committee, and American Jewish Congress passed from the older generation of philanthropists to a younger group of professionally trained social workers and attorneys.

Will Maslow, a lawyer, headed the American Jewish Congress. He arrived in the United States at age six and grew up in "a Jewish socialist-labor background." He became a full-time professional in civil rights work and broadened the work of the American Jewish Congress beyond strictly Jewish issues. He credited his membership on President Roosevelt's Fair Employment Practices Committee in 1943 as providing his "first real contact with the problems of discrimination against Negroes." John Slawson, who immigrated to America at the age of seven and later studied social work at Columbia University, took over the leadership of the American Jewish Committee in 1943. He applied the principles of modern psychology to combat discrimination and prejudice.

Scholars working for both the American Jewish Congress and American Jewish Committee attacked racist thinking by offering scientific proof of the psychological origins of racial prejudice and religious discrimination. The new activism included highly structured public campaigns against prejudice. Radio and television announcements, posters, school materials, books, and magazine articles proliferated. The movie based on Laura Z. Hobson's popular novel about anti-Semitism, *Gentlemen's Agreement*, won the 1947 Academy Award for best picture.

Jewish defense groups, including the American Jewish Committee, understood the need to broaden the fight against bigotry and intolerance to include everyone. After World War II the committee and the American Jewish Congress turned their focus from exclusively Jewish concerns to more general social action. Both groups expanded their network of local community relations councils established during the war. The American Jewish Congress created the Commission of Law and Social Action. Aware that its membership consisted of Jews who lived in the North and the South, an Executive Committee resolution fearlessly took a stand against discrimination. "It's proper ...that the American Jewish Committee join with other groups in the protection of the civil rights of the members of all groups irrespective of race, religion, color or national origin...."

Building on the small movement toward integration begun during World War II, attention of blacks and Jews turned to Washington and to Franklin Roosevelt's successor. President Harry S. Truman was dismayed by the growing number of lynchings of blacks in the South. In 1946, he appointed a Committee on Civil

Rights to study America's pressing racial problem. Serving on the committee were Rabbi Roland B. Gittlesohn, of Boston's Temple Israel, and Morris Ernst, a Jewish civil rights attorney. "I want our Bill of Rights implemented in fact," President Truman said, "We have been trying to do this for 150 years. We are making progress, but we are not making progress fast enough." Among those testifying before the committee was John Slawson of the American Jewish Committee. He proposed the elimination of the poll tax which discouraged poor African-Americans from voting. In 1947, less than 12 percent of blacks in the Deep South met strict voting qualifications. He called for enactment of legislation to halt the continued lynchings. He also suggested that the government begin its civil rights crusade by concentrating on the educational and legal arenas.

A year later—the same year in which Jackie Robinson broke the color barrier to become the first African-American major league baseball player—the committee issued its report "To Secure These Rights." "We have considered what government's appropriate role should be in the securing of our rights and have concluded that it must assume greater leadership. We believe that the time for action is now. Our recommendations for bringing the United States closer to its historic goal follow." The main goal of the historic document was to eliminate segregation based on race, color, creed, or national origin from American life. Specifically, the committee's report focused on two major areas. In employment, the report recommended the establishment of a federal Fair Employment Practice Act. In education, the report called for the elimination of discrimination in the admission of students to universities.

In February, 1948, President Truman sent Congress a ten-point civil rights program and issued an executive order eliminating discrimination on federal property. A month later, A. Philip Randolph led a delegation to a meeting with Truman to urge the end of discrimination in the military. "In my recent travels around the country," he told the president, "I found Negroes in no mood to shoulder guns for democracy abroad while they are denied democracy here at home." Drawing on the success of his planned march on Washington in 1941, Randolph told the president that he was prepared to lead a "campaign of civil disobedience" in the country. "We will relentlessly wage war on the Jim Crow armed forces program" and "fill up the jails."

On July 26, 1948, President Truman issued Executive Order 9981 which stated, "There shall be equality of treatment and opportunity for all persons in the armed services without regard to race, color, religion or national origin." In addition, he issued a second Executive Order, 9980, which set up a Presidential Committee on Equality of Treatment and Opportunity.

Threats of marches and civil disobedience brought some relief. Presidential decrees also helped. Yet by 1950, African-Americans had not gained much equality with whites. The nation largely continued to be segregated by race. The major advances in civil rights were won in the courts.

From its inception, the NAACP realized the importance of legal action. Arthur Spingarn and the other attorneys who volunteered their time and talents dur-

117

ing the NAACP's early years were, by the mid-1930s, replaced by a staff of paid lawyers. For tax reasons, the NAACP transferred its legal department to a separate agency in 1940, the NAACP Legal Defense and Educational Fund, with Arthur Spingarn assuming the position of president and Thurgood Marshall, a thirty-year-old African-American lawyer, as Chief Counsel. At a time when there were few African-American lawyers in America, Thurgood Marshall succeeded Charles Houston, another African-American who was the first paid General Counsel of the NAACP.

Civil rights leaders in front of the White House after meeting with President Truman. Among the leaders were Benjamin Epstein of the Anti-Defamation League, Adolph Held of the Jewish Labor Committee, David Solomon of the Jewish War Veterans, A. Philip Randolph, Felix Cohen of the American Jewish Congress, and Roy Wilkins of the NAACP. (Archives of Labor and Urban Affairs, Wayne State University)

Marshall and the NAACP attorneys successfully brought pivotal cases before the Supreme Court. They fought housing restrictions, persuading the Court in a 1948 decision in Shelley v. Kraemer to declare that housing covenants could not be enforced since they denied "equality in the enjoyment of property rights" and thereby violated the Fourth Amendment to the United States Constitution. They fought voting restrictions. A Texas law stated, "In no event shall a Negro be eligible to participate in a Democratic primary election." When the Supreme Court overturned that law, Texas passed a revised law which continued to deny blacks the same right. Thurgood Marshall returned the case to the Supreme Court in 1944. The Court struck down the new law, saying, "the right to vote in a primary is a right secured by the Constitution."

A small number of civil rights lawyers worked for the major Jewish "defense" organizations—the American Jewish Congress, the Anti-Defamation League, and the American Jewish Committee. Together with the Legal Defense Fund and the American Civil Liberties Union, they employed more civil rights attorneys than the federal government. While the legal antennae of the Jewish defense groups were tuned to cases which affected Jewish Americans, their concern was with every case that threatened the rights of all. When asked why Jews were so concerned with civil rights questions, Supreme Court Justice Felix Frankfurter responded, "One who belongs to the most vilified and persecuted minority in history is not likely to be insensitive to the freedoms guaranteed by the Constitution."

One example of such a case involved an Oregon law, inspired by the Ku Klux Klan, that prohibited the operation of parochial schools in that state. While aimed specifically at the large number of Roman Catholic schools, schools operated by other religious groups were also in danger. Although there were hardly any such Jewish schools in Oregon at the time, Louis Marshall filed a brief on behalf of the American Jewish Committee.

Meanwhile, local branches of Jewish organizations worked with state legislatures to pass pro-civil rights laws. In New Jersey, eight bills written by the New Jersey branch of the American Jewish Congress and sponsored by the state's Joint Council for Civil Rights passed. The new laws prohibited discrimination in public and publicly assisted housing. In 1954, the American Jewish Congress filed the first brief in the North, which ended de-facto segregation in Englewood, New Jersey.

Lawyers from the major Jewish defense organizations participated in the important civil rights cases of the 1940s and 1950s. They joined in many of the Legal Defense Fund cases as *amici curiae*—friends of the court. Each hard-won case put a dent in the seemingly solid wall of discrimination.

In spite of the legal successes, civil rights attorneys knew that the key to striking down the evils of segregation rested on overturning the "separate but equal" ruling embodied in the Plessy v. Ferguson case of 1896. Realizing that a direct challenge to that ruling could not succeed, the NAACP whittled away at "separate but equal" in a series of smaller cases. Since the courts made decisions based on previous rulings, each newly won segregation case provided a legal precedent on which to build succeeding cases.

The first education cases dealt with graduate schools and universities. In 1936 Thurgood Marshall and Charles Houston won Pearson v. Murray in the Maryland courts. The case revolved around Maryland's refusal to admit Murray, an African-American, to a state law school. When the state agreed to pay his

Thurgood Marshall. (NAACP Legal Defense and Educational Fund)

tuition at a northern law school, Murray refused. In 1938, the NAACP won when the United States Supreme Court ruled against the state of Missouri in a case similar to Mr. Murray's. The ruling declared that states must admit blacks to white universities when no comparable black institution exists.

In 1948, Thurgood Marshall argued McLaurin v. Oklahoma before the Supreme Court. That year, George McLaurin, a sixty-eight-year-old African-American applied to graduate school at the University of Oklahoma. The state finally admitted Mr. McLaurin to law school but assigned him to an anteroom that opened into the classroom occupied by whites. But winning that battle did not mean the end of the conflict for Mr. McLaurin. While the state reassigned him into the white classroom, it also provided him with separate seating there, in the library, and the cafeteria. In 1950, the Supreme Court finally ruled in the same case that African-American graduate students cannot be segregated from other students since they must "receive the same treatment at the hands of the state as students of other races."

The American Jewish Congress filed briefs in the McLaurin case and in Sweatt v. Painter, another graduate school case involving the assignment of a Texas African-American to a "Negro" law school hastily opened in a state building basement. It was separate from the state's white law school but far from equal. The Supreme Court ruled that "Jim Crow" graduate schools were not the same as "real" schools.

Jewish defense organizations were involved in many of the trailblazing civil rights cases leading to the overturn of the "separate but equal" doctrine. The ADL, American Jewish Committee, and the American Jewish Congress received opposition from some southern members who feared public reaction against Jews in their communities. But the national organizations did not hesitate to continue their strong legal support of civil rights cases and legislation. In an internal memo, an American Jewish Committee official wrote, "I think it of great importance that we have a talk about a program which would educate our southern friends as to our broad civil rights policy . . . Inasmuch as we will probably concern ourselves with other matters which involve Negroes in the South, we should formulate our approach at the earliest opportunity."

After winning a succession of cases before the Supreme Court, the NAACP Legal Defense Fund was ready to make its final assault on Plessy v. Ferguson. Jack Greenberg, who as a young Legal Defense Fund (LDF) lawyer worked with Thurgood Marshall, later remarked, "We had won our graduate and professional school cases—now it was onward—toward an end to all segregation—and downward—to colleges, high schools and grade schools." By 1952 the Supreme Court had a variety of school segregation cases before it. The long-awaited overturn of "Plessy v. Ferguson" and its "separate but equal" ruling was close at hand.

TO THE STREETS

"Turn on the hoses!"

Bull Connor

Topeka, Kansas seemed to be the most unlikely place from which to launch a civil-rights revolution in the United States. Kansas was not in the Deep South and had not been in the Confederacy during the Civil War. Yet, the city's elementary schools were segregated: African-American children were bused to distant black schools rather than allowed to attend neighborhood white schools. The families of several children objected and with the help of the NAACP brought suit against the Topeka Board of Education. Oliver Brown headed the alphabetical list of parents. The rest is history.

Brown v. Board of Education became the pivotal civil rights case of the twentieth century. It quickly made its way up from the Kansas state courts, which sided with the board, to the United States Supreme Court. "Why," asked chief NAACP lawyer Thurgood Marshall, "of all of the multitudinous groups of people in this country do you have to single out Negroes and give them this separate treatment?" Working with Marshall was a young Legal Defense Fund attorney, Jack Greenberg. Later, when Marshall was appointed to the Supreme Court, Greenberg succeeded him as head of the fund.

Jack Greenberg was born in New York City in 1924. After receiving his law degree from Columbia University, he began work with the NAACP Legal Defense Fund, eventually succeeding Thurgood Marshall as chief counsel from 1961 to 1984. He then returned to Columbia University first as vice-dean of the Law School and in 1989 as dean of Columbia College. As a civil rights lawyer for the NAACP he was directly involved in the landmark legal cases in school integration, equal employment, fair housing, and voter registration.

On May 17, 1954, the historic decision of the Supreme Court was announced. Voting 9 to 0, the Court effectively removed the major legal stumbling block to equality. Brown v. Board of Education replaced Plessy v. Ferguson: separate but equal was no longer a legal mandate. One law school dean called the decision the "most important governmental act of any kind since the Emancipation Proclamation."

Footnotes to the decision credited the work of Dr. Kenneth Clark, an African-American psychologist who conducted experiments with children using black and

Jack Greenberg. (NAACP Legal and Educational Fund)

white dolls. The tests proved that self-esteem of black children suffered in a segregrated society by generating a "feeling of inferiority as to their status in the community." The children thought of the white dolls as "nice" and the black dolls as "bad." Much of Dr. Clark's research was done originally for the American Jewish Committee since both the committee and the American Jewish Congress utilized the social sciences to fight discrimination. Their research provided the Court with the "modern authority" with which to overturn Plessy v. Ferguson.

The Court urged the implementation of integration "with all deliberate speed." The South interpreted the Court's opinion as an excuse for delay in implementa-

127

tion. Although schools in border states were quickly integrated, few schools in the Deep South were integrated ten years after the Court decision.

Both the Anti-Defamation League and the American Jewish Committee filed *amici curiae* briefs in the Brown case. Of the six lawyers signing the Brown v. Board of Education brief, five were Jewish. The case might never have happened without the courage of a Brown not related to the plaintiff. Esther Brown was a Jewish resident of Kansas City who became outraged at the educational conditions of African-American children. She became an activist, prodding the black community to rally in support of improved schools and learning conditions. She toured the state raising money for legal costs and to support the private schools set up by the African-American community as they boycotted the inferior public schools. Recognizing the importance of this Topeka situation in the fight for truly equal education, Esther Brown contacted Thurgood Marshall. The NAACP lawyers, including Jack Greenberg, would carry the case all the way to the United States Supreme Court. Speaking of Esther Brown, the secretary of the Topeka branch of the NAACP said, "I don't know if we could have done it without her."

When the decision was announced, Jewish religious groups quickly responded. The Union of American Hebrew Congregations issued a statement urging all members to use "their influence to secure acceptance and implementation of the desegregation decisions in every community in our land." Conservative rabbis attending their annual convention adopted a resolution praising the Court stating that the "unanimity of their act and its courage will leave its indelible stamp not only on our country but the entire world."

Reaction from the South was immediate. Hate groups such as the Ku Klux Klan and newly spawned White Citizen's Councils went into action. The governors of southern states implemented a continuing succession of delay tactics. Bigots of all stripes surfaced to foment hatred against blacks and Jews, a vulnerable minority comprising less than 1 percent of the population in the South and visible as main street merchants or professionals. As during the Civil War, most southern Jews tended to publicly identify with the views of their white neighbors. Whatever inner feelings on segregation they may have had, they wanted nothing more than to blend into the background and not call attention to themselves. But a revival of anti-Jewish sentiment among hard-core segregationists made it difficult for Jews to remain anonymous in the hate-filled atmosphere.

As national Jewish organizations became more visible in the fight against segregation, southern Jews feared an upsurge in anti-Semitism. The American Jewish Committee and the Anti-Defamation League continued to publish pamphlets and produce films and radio and television spots in order to educate Americans about discrimination. Working with the NAACP, the American Jewish Congress issued a 1953 statement on "Civil Rights in the United States." They investigated the work of hate groups and publicized their findings. Locally in the South, rabbis spoke out against the hate and fear which surrounded them. One rabbi, speaking about the newly organized White Citizen's Council in his community, admonished his congregants, "let the name of no Jew be found on the roster of these hate organizations."

Rabbis in the North and South used their influence to strengthen convergent support of civil rights. Many rabbis joined with their liberal colleagues, Jewish and Christian, to affect legislation, speak out against injustice, and create social action projects for their congregants. One rabbi, speaking before a Protestant congregation in 1957, said, "If we don't rise above our partisan feelings of segregation versus integration, we'll have disintegration in our public schools." Another rabbi testified before the Arkansas senate against segregationist bills. "Above my love for Arkansas," he told the legislators, "comes my devotion to America. I regard the Supreme Court as the final democratic authority of the land."

A year after Brown v. Board of Education, the fight for civil rights took a dramatic step out of the courtroom and into the streets. The battle, until now fought by a small group of liberal legislators and lawyers, was now joined by hundreds of thousands of whites and blacks dissatisfied with the status quo. Their nonviolent revolution was led by groups of local blacks—many young—not afraid to take matters into their own hands.

It was in Montgomery, Alabama, where the tactic of nonviolence was first used in the civil rights struggle. Rosa Parks, forty-two years old, was tired. After a hard day's work, she boarded a city bus in Montgomery on December 1, 1955. Local law dictated that whites and blacks were to be separated, not only at drinking fountains, restaurants, schools, hospitals, and parks but on buses too. Blacks sat in the rear; whites in front. Ms. Parks sat down in an available seat and removed her tight shoes. A few stops later, a white man boarded the crowded bus. There was standing room only and the man demanded the seat from Rosa Parks. Politely, she answered, "No, I'm sorry." She was arrested and taken to jail.

The newly arrived minister at the Dexter Avenue Baptist Church, Dr. Martin Luther King, Jr., a graduate of Boston University's School of Theology, told an overflow crowd that had gathered to support Rosa Parks, "We are tired of being segregated and humiliated.... We have no alternative but to protest," he said, "but there will be no threats and intimidation."

For one year, the African-American residents of Montgomery, Alabama, boycotted the city's bus system. While they peacefully walked or arranged for private transportation, the bus company suffered economically. The black community was struck by escalating violence. Bombs shattered churches and the homes of ministers. Dr. King's house was bombed on January 30, 1956, but there were no casualties. In February Dr. King and dozens of other prominent blacks were arrested and charged with conspiracy to conduct an illegal boycott. Rather than dissuading the black community, these acts strengthened the resolve to continue with the boycott. Across America people watched and most sympathized with the boycotters. In December 1956 a Supreme Court decision declared segregation of buses in Montgomery to be unconstitutional. The persistence of the black citizens of Montgomery and their adherence to nonviolence resulted in more than the desegregation of the buses. It demonstrated the power of nonviolent protest.

The Jews of the South viewed the increasing agitation with great alarm. They were, after all, a vulnerable minority. While a few actually joined White Citizens' Councils, most southern Jews preferred to maintain a low public profile. One rabbi explained that Jews "depend upon the good-will of their non-Jewish neighbors for survival." Other rabbis in the South understood the dangers too but were outspoken in their support of the rights of African-Americans. The Board of the Union of American Hebrew Congregations issued a resolution in 1958 on behalf of those rabbis who "reacted to the trials and heart-rending conflicts of the struggle for human equality in their area with courage and with fortitude. Their words and deeds are precious to us..."

But some of their neighbors were not so understanding. Even as bombings escalated at African-American homes and churches, temples across the South were also targeted by the dynamite-wielding bigots. On November 11, 1957, an attempt was made to bomb Temple Beth-El in Charleston, South Carolina. On March 16, 1958, $30,000 worth of damage was inflicted on the school building of a temple in Miami, Florida. That same day another bomb destroyed the Jewish Community Center in Nashville, Tennessee. On April 28, a bomb was discovered at a temple in Birmingham, Alabama, before it could go off. An African-American church in the same city was not so fortunate. Five children died in a cowardly bombing.

Accompanying the violence was a dramatic increase in anti-Semitism. Hate-filled literature was distributed across the South. "Desegregation is a Zionist-Communist plot," one tract read, "to mongrelize the white race so that the Jews can take over." In such an atmosphere, nervous southern Jews urged their rabbis not to "arouse the ire of those in a position to harm the Jews." Among those rabbis who would not be silenced were three who put their lives in danger, spoke the truth as they believed it, and saw their temples bombed.

Rabbi Jacob M. Rothschild of Atlanta told his congregants in 1948 that "unless decent people take up the burden, the South faces a return to the most primitive kind of bigotry and race hatred." He called on his congregants to "be among those who are willing to do something" to bring peace to the South. In 1957 he joined with other Atlanta clergy to issue the "Atlanta Manifesto" on securing rights for African-Americans. A year later his temple was rocked by a dynamite blast that did $200,000 worth of damage. Ralph McGill of the *Atlanta Constitution* wrote, "You do not preach and encourage hatred for the Negro and hope to restrict it to that field." Rabbi Rothschild looked on the positive side. "The bombing," he said, "created a reaction of such outrage that it backfired." Atlantans, disgusted by the violence, began talking openly about ways to solve the race problem peacefully.

In Jackson, Mississippi, where 400 Jews lived among 150,000 Christians, Rabbi Perry Nussbaum of Beth Israel Synagogue did not remain silent. Born in Mississippi, he spoke up publicly against segregation but not without fear. "Sometimes," he later recalled, "you were sure your phone was tapped. You wondered about some of the mail, delivered and undelivered..." Another Mississippi colleague, Rabbi Charles Mantinband of Hattiesburg, was perhaps the most outspoken of the southern Jewish clergy. He was raised in Virginia and attended segregated schools. As a rabbi serving congregations in the South, he worked to improve racial conditions. With a population of 50,000, Hattiesburg had a Jewish population of less than 175. In spite of the numbers, Rabbi Mantinband told his congregants, "Mississippi Jews cannot resign from the Jewish people." He engaged non-Jews in biblical debates to debunk any charges that the Bible condoned segregation of the races. At a time when African-Americans and whites did not mix socially, he openly invited blacks to his home. With his life constantly under threat, Rabbi Mantinband remained the only member of a small group of like-minded clergy in Mississippi not driven from his pulpit. He once plaintively ended a letter to a friend "from one who doesn't want to be a hero."

The teaching and leadership of Martin Luther King, Jr. attracted support from many who followed his belief in nonviolence as the only way to win rights. In May 1957, Dr. King organized other like-minded ministers into the Southern Christian Leadership Conference. Brought into national prominence by the power of his message and the continuing television coverage, Martin Luther King, Jr. became the leader of the black civil rights movement. Soon, the spirit of nonviolent protest overtook the South and brought about a revolution in civil rights. Organized and united in nonviolence,

African-Americans prepared to bring change to their own lives.

One of Dr. Martin Luther King, Jr.'s first appearances before a Jewish congregation was on May 3, 1957. Rabbi Edward E. Klein, a long-time civil rights activist, invited Dr. King to preach at the Friday evening service of the Stephen Wise Free Synagogue in New York on "The Future of Integration." *The New York Post* reported that the congregation had to control its desire to applaud during the solemn religious service. "I cannot tell you what it meant to all of us," Rabbi Klein wrote later to Dr. King. "Our congregation was more moved by your message than I can say.... You moved their hearts and minds in such a way that their hands have been prompted to serve the cause of justice and love for all regardless of race and creed."

On February 1, 1960, four African-American freshmen at North Carolina Agricultural and Technical College walked into the Greensboro Woolworth's store and sat down at the lunch counter. With full knowledge that they were breaking local law that segregated blacks from whites, they nonetheless waited in vain to be served. Sit-ins, the next wave of nonviolent protest, began. The tactic called for nonviolent direct action to protest segregation in restaurants, libraries, and other public places.

Other organizations, led mainly by young black students, such as the Congress on Racial Equality (CORE) and the Student Non-Violent Coordinating Committee (SNCC), trained young activists in the principles of nonviolent action. The sit-in technique was embraced by young African-Americans across the South and

135

lunch counters in chain stores throughout the South were targets. The tactic spread spontaneously to local movie theaters, swimming pools, and libraries. Southern white reaction was uncompromising. The young protesters were seen as lawbreakers and troublemakers, incited by outsiders. Mass arrests of demonstrators quickly followed. The students could not be stopped: jail sentences only heightened their assertion of constitutional rights.

Funds were raised to provide bail money and legal costs. Volunteer lawyers, many from Jewish organizations around the nation, headed South to aid the students. Staff members of the American Jewish Committee "passed the hat" in their offices and raised $335 which was sent directly to Thurgood Marshall at the NAACP Legal Defense Fund. In an accompanying letter they stated their support of the demonstrations as a "most impressive display of human dignity and courage." Just a few years earlier, the national president of the American Jewish Committee had chastised those southern members who urged less activism. "Jews cannot buy security or status for themselves," he wrote, "in an atmosphere where injustice is tolerated."

A 1961 resolution by the Jewish Labor Committee stated admiration for "the determined yet restrained and non-violent manner which the Negro community has taken the offensive in behalf of civil rights and human dignity." Beginning in 1955, the Jewish Labor Committee sponsored an annual conference on civil rights for all trade unions. At the 1958 gathering, Roy Wilkins, the Executive Secretary of the NAACP, stated, "The White Citizen's Councils were born in Mississippi in 1954. Their original call to arms and the literature were not only anti-Negro but anti-Semitic."

By the early 1960s over nine hundred demonstrations were held in eleven southern states. Older civil rights leaders, who were first taken aback by the brazen tactics of nonviolence, could only cheer on the newcomers. "Don't stop," Arthur Spingarn of the NAACP told them, "don't delay. The time for advance is always now!"

Support groups arose on northern college campuses. People found it difficult to accept the fact that while African-Americans were welcome to spend money in southern stores, they could not sit at the dining counters. The publisher of the *Carolina Israelite* newspaper, Harry Golden, provided a humorous solution to the problem. His "vertical plan" called for the removal of all seats from lunch counters and schools since whites did not seem to mind if blacks stood next to them.

National chain stores such as F. W. Woolworth, Kress, and McCrory were picketed in northern cities in sympathy for the sit-ins of young black activists in those stores' southern branches. Southern cities in the border states yielded to the tactic and desegregated some facilities. In the Deep South, however, the non-violence of the demonstrators was met with arrests, snarling police dogs, beatings, and gassings. By September, 1961, over 3,600 students had been arrested.

In some southern communities, clergy and responsible civic leaders worked quietly in the background to mediate between the protesters and the store owners. The American Jewish Committee used its influence to

Stores were picketed in the North to support southern desegregation efforts. (Archives of Labor and Urban Affairs, Wayne State University)

arrange talks with the owners of Jewish-controlled stores. To avoid repercussions, those meetings were held in the "strictest confidentiality."

Since its founding, the American Jewish Committee had always preferred "a position of negotiation and conciliation" over direct confrontation. Its founding statement proclaimed that "Jews cannot ensure equality for themselves until and unless it is assured for all." A 1963 statement brought that principle up to date by adding that the denial of basic human rights to African-Americans is not "a Negro problem but...a challenge calling for a moral commitment by Americans of every race and religion...." In an official statement adopted in 1960 at its 53rd Annual Meeting, the committee affirmed its support of the demonstrations and the "principle that there shall be no discrimination where food is offered for sale to the public."

Dr. Joachim Prinz, the national president of the American Jewish Congress, issued a statement to his staff on March 25, 1960, in support of the sit-ins. "We do not accept the thesis," he said, "that businesses may solicit the patronage of Negro customers in all other departments and deny them the right to equal service in the consumption of food and beverage....We support that call and add our voice." He urged all members to write to the major national department stores—Woolworth, Kress, Kresge, and Grant's—in support of the sit-ins. In addition, American Jewish Congress members held a highly-publicized picket line in front of the Woolworth store on Fifth Avenue in New York City.

Prinz personally wrote to the presidents of the department stores urging them "to revise your policy so that these stores treat alike all law-abiding customers regardless of their race or color." In response, the president of S. S. Kresge Company candidly told Prinz, "We cannot condemn the objectives of the sit-downers, nor in general the orderly conduct of their passive resistance campaign. This poses a grave dilemma.... We are earnestly seeking a way out of this dilemma and we are actively working with other responsible organizations and agencies with the hope that through community interest on a city by city basis we may help to solve this complex problem."

Demonstrations against segregated facilities were not limited to the Deep South. For generations, the Gwynne Oak Amusement Park in Baltimore, Maryland, was a favorite picnic and amusement destination for white families; blacks were not allowed. Picketing began early in 1963, culminating in massive nonviolent protests during the week of the Fourth of July, leading to the arrest of nearly four hundred demonstrators. Among the picketers was Michael Schwerner, who was murdered two years later while working for civil rights in Mississippi. When Rabbi Morris Lieberman was arrested at the park he said, "I think every American should celebrate the Fourth of July!" The park was finally integrated on August 28.

Jews had been involved with the activities of the National Association for the Advancement of Colored People since its founding in 1909. Beginning with the Montgomery bus boycott, Jews expanded their involvement by allying themselves with the newer black organizations such as CORE and SNCC. Nearly three-quarters of the financial support for these newer groups came from Jewish contributors. Jews were also involved in more direct ways as speechwriters, lawyers, and fund-raisers.

Staff members of the Jewish defense organizations also worked directly with governmental agencies. Robert Greene, an area director of the American Jewish Com-

mittee, joined a White House–sponsored team to desegregate restaurants along a major highway in Maryland.

Like most civil rights regulations enacted by the
federal government, the 1955 ruling of the Interstate
Commerce Commission outlawing segregation on
buses that traveled across state lines was also ignored
by most communities in the Deep South. Compliance
did not materialize even with the 1960 Supreme Court
decision in Boynton v. Virginia, which declared that
segregated waiting rooms and restaurants serving
interstate passengers were indeed unconstitutional.
Encouraged by the national reaction to sit-ins, the
Congress of Racial Equality decided to test implementation of the interstate bus rules in light of the
Supreme Court ruling. On May 4, 1961, a mixed group
of thirteen young people, trained in nonviolent tactics,
boarded two buses—a Greyhound and a Trailways—in
Washington, D.C., headed for New Orleans, Louisiana.

Crossing the Mason-Dixon Line, the "Freedom Riders" first met with little resistance from white
supremacists. Not until the buses reached the Deep
South did conditions become life-threatening. As the
Greyhound bus pulled into the bus station in Anniston, Alabama, it was quickly surrounded by an armed
mob wielding knives and bats, who broke bus windows
and slashed at the tires. No police were in sight, so the
bus fled with fifty carloads of local toughs in close pur-
suit. Just outside of town the tires blew up and the bus
veered off the road and into a ditch where it was surrounded by the hostile pursuers.

Rocks smashed the bus windows. Amid the escalating jeers and threats, someone in the crowd threw a

firebomb into the bus. The Freedom Riders tumbled out of the bus to escape the inferno and were met with the blows of fists and clubs. The mob severely beat the riders until many of them lay unconscious and bloody on the ground. The Trailways bus arrived in Anniston an hour later. Informed of the fate of their colleagues, they too were beaten by hoodlums who stormed onto the bus before the driver cautiously maneuvered the vehicle through back roads to Birmingham. There, waiting reporters watched as bloodied riders tumbled out of the bus. As an unruly mob surrounded them, the riders entered the "Whites Only" waiting room to seek protection from the segregationist mob. Only a thin line of police officers protected them. Sheriff "Bull" Connor ordered the Freedom Riders arrested under "protective custody." Radio and television coverage of the Anniston and Birmingham violence flashed across the world. Shaken by the violence and the indifference of local police, leaders of CORE decided to suspend the rides. Instead, an independent group of young people from the Nashville Student Non-Violent Coordinating Committee continued the project.

Arriving in Montgomery, Alabama, on Saturday morning, May 20, 1961, the new group was set upon by an angry mob of 1,000. Although local police had been informed of the bus's arrival, they were nowhere to be seen, in spite of the governor's insistence that he did not need any outside help to keep law and order. The riders were beaten with pipes and chains, as were reporters and photographers. Twenty-one were injured, some severely. A deputy sent by United States Attorney General Robert Kennedy, brother of the president,was rendered unconscious. The riders sought refuge in the First Baptist Church where the next day over 1,000 African-Americans were to gather at a mass meeting to hear Dr. Martin Luther King, Jr.

On Sunday, as people gathered peacefully inside, an angry chanting crowd, wielding weapons and clubs and hurling firebombs, gathered outside. Informed of the potential for a great disaster and the unwillingness of local police to protect the people in the church, President Kennedy immediately ordered four hundred armed federal marshals to Montgomery to keep the peace. They arrived just in time to prevent the church from being overrun by the furious mob. Across America and the world people watched their televisions as the violence unfolded before their eyes.

The Freedom Riders next headed to Jackson, Mississippi, where they were arrested and immediately sentenced to sixty days in jail. Convinced of the righteousness of their actions, many decided to stay in jail rather than post bail. Even behind bars, they remained a visible and vocal presence. Their goal was to fill up every jail in the South. They were following the words of Martin Luther King, Jr., who said, "The way of the passive resister is the way of sacrifice. It may mean going to jail...." The American Jewish Congress called on Robert Kennedy to intervene as "friend of the court" for the twenty-seven jailed Freedom Fighters. The congress also urged members to write to the Attorney General and to join with their local CORE chapters to protect the rights of Freedom Riders. Across the country, hundreds of young people trained to become

Freedom Riders. Professors at Ivy League colleges and well-known members of the clergy boarded buses along with black and white students. The Union of American Hebrew Congregations told members in June, "It is essential that there be direct Jewish reli-

Rabbi Martin Freedman (right) and Rabbi Israel Dresner were taken to the Tallahassee, Florida city building, where they were charged with unlawful assembly after they and ten other "Freedom Riders" were arrested attempting to eat at the Tallahassee airport restaurant. (American Jewish Archives)

gious participation in the bus rides." Nearly two-thirds of all white Freedom Riders were Jewish.

In Washington, Robert Kennedy persuaded the Interstate Commerce Commission to order the removal of all "Colored Only" and "White Only" signs in buses and terminals. The sit-ins and freedom rides were followed by wade-ins, pray-ins, buy-ins, and swim-ins—attempts to provide African-Americans with full equality with white citizens in all public facilities, North and South. While the early successes were important, they also strengthened the resolve of segregationists to fight back. A new phase of the struggle was set to begin.

THANK GOD ALMIGHTY

"The plight of the Negro must become our
most important concern."

Rabbi Abraham Joshua Heschel

Dr. Martin Luther King, Jr. was the architect of the nonviolent civil rights movement. Dr. Abraham Joshua Heschel was its Jewish conscience. Born in Warsaw, Poland, in 1907 into a family of Jewish Hasidic scholars, young Abraham quickly demonstrated his own learning abilities in the study of Jewish texts. He was ordained as a rabbi while still in his teens and moved on to the University of Berlin. "In those months I went through moments of profound bitterness," he recalled. It was painful for him to reconcile his fervent religious beliefs with the study of philosophy. Slowly, he began to realize that his Hasidic background provided the foundation from which to engage the secular world. In 1933, shortly before the Nazis came to power, he received his doctorate in philosophy. His first book—a collection of Yiddish poetry—was quickly followed by works on Maimonides and the Prophets and earned him a deserved reputation as a serious Jewish scholar.

He was arrested by the Gestapo in 1938 and deported to Poland. A month before the outbreak of World War II, Heschel fled to England and in 1940 was invited to teach at Hebrew Union College in Cincinnati, Ohio, the rabbinical training school of Reform Judaism. He would always be grateful to the Reform movement for saving him from the Holocaust. But at age thirty-three, with limited abilities in English, he felt uncomfortable away from his traditional religious roots. In 1945 he accepted an invitation from the Jewish Theological Seminary of America to come to New York and join the faculty of Conservative Judaism's primary institution. There he remained for twenty-seven years until his death in 1972.

His lifelong study of the biblical prophets deeply affected his commitment to activism. When the civil rights movement developed in the late 1950s, Heschel responded not only with words but with deeds. His understanding of Judaism was based on the belief that religious thoughts must be accompanied by righteous actions in the secular world. Echoing the earlier thoughts and deeds of Rabbis David Einhorn and Stephen S. Wise, Heschel said, "I've learned from the prophets that I have to be involved in the affairs of man, in the affairs of suffering man. And I would like to say that one of the saddest things about contemporary life in America is that the prophets are unknown." "Prophecy," he later wrote, "is the voice that God has lent to the silent agony, a voice to the plundered poor. ...It is a form of living." Like the ancient prophets, Rabbi Heschel reacted to the needs of the world with deeds of social action. "By performance of sacred deeds," he wrote, "we concretize our faith in God; we justify God's faith in us." To him, the separation of religious and secular life provided "a wall...between the conscience and God."

To Heschel, fighting for the rights of others was simply an extension of his religious obligations. "The Negro Movement is an outcry of pain in which a sickness of our total society comes to expression." "The issue," he wrote, "is whether we are morally strong, whether we are spiritually worthy to answer God's demand." His sense of humor was never far from the serious nature of his message. "The idea of judging a person in terms of black or brown or white is an eye disease," he told a television interviewer.

Heschel was not a tall man but his shock of unruly hair and prominent beard gave him the appearance of a prophet of old. "Father Abraham" was the name given him by those he met at civil rights marches and demonstrations. He was outspoken no matter where he appeared. He told one group, "it was easier for the children of Israel to cross the Red Sea than for the Civil Rights legislation to pass the floor of the United States Senate." At a conference on race and religion in Chicago he said, "Equality as a religious command-ment means personal involvement, fellowship, mutual reverence and concern. It means my being hurt when a

Negro is offended. It means my being hurt whenever a Negro is disfranchised." His daughter Susannah told of the time Heschel chastised Jesuit priests in Germany for not doing more to save Jews during the Holocaust. They explained their outward indifference by saying they feared the Nazis would close their beloved library. Heschel responded bitterly. "Can you imagine, measuring books against human beings!"

He developed a close relationship with Martin Luther King, Jr. and became the best-known rabbi in the civil rights movement. Heschel's teachings inspired other rabbis. He urged his colleagues, "Daily we should take account and ask: what have I done today to alleviate the anguish, to mitigate the evil, to prevent humiliation?" In April 1963, Martin Luther King, Jr. led a series of demonstrations, boycotts, and marches in Birmingham, Alabama, a city that resisted any liberalization of Jim Crow laws and attitudes. Facing the nonviolent demonstrators were the snarling police dogs and high-pressure water hoses of police commissioner "Bull" Connor. Each day, news reports around the country carried graphic descriptions of the violent police reactions. The sight of singing and marching young people attacked by dogs and high-pressure fire hoses shocked Americans. King was arrested and wrote his epic "Letter from Birmingham Jail," which became a rallying document for the civil rights movement.

News of the Birmingham struggle reached Conservative rabbis assembled at their annual Rabbinical Assembly convention. In response to the brutality, a group of nineteen rabbis was quickly dispatched to

150

Rabbi Abraham Joshua Heschel presents award to Rev. Martin Luther King, Jr. (Library of Congress)

Birmingham as official representatives of the assembled rabbis. Their mission was "to speak and to act on behalf of human rights and dignity." Unwelcome at white motels, they squeezed into the black motel where Dr. King was living. They attended prayer services in black churches. To emphasize their presence as Jews, the rabbis wore their yarmulkes or skullcaps wherever they went. Soon, everyone wanted to wear a "Freedom Cap." A call went out for thousands of skullcaps, which became a sign of honor among young

African-American marchers in future marches. "Wherever the freedom movement is," one youth said, "God is to be found."

A. Philip Randolph was no stranger to mass marches on Washington. In 1963, with civil rights legislation pending in Congress, he called for another. With the help and support of the major civil rights organizations, a march on Washington was planned for August 28 to pressure for passage of a comprehensive civil rights bill to enforce equality in public accommodations, education, voting rights, and housing. Among groups prominently supporting the march were the American Jewish Committee, the American Jewish Congress, the Anti-Defamation League of B'nai B'rith, the Jewish Labor Committee, and rabbis from Orthodox, Conservative, and Reform congregations. The American Jewish Committee told members, "where one minority suffers, no minority group can feel permanently secure."

Volunteers from labor unions and churches worked together to insure the success of the massive march. In New York, Catholic nuns, staff members of the Jewish Theological Seminary, and students at the Union Theological Seminary gathered to make thousands of bag lunches for the demonstrators. The International Ladies Garment Workers Union paid bus and train fares for thousands of members.

At the Jewish Theological Seminary all staff were given permission to leave work to participate in the march. For those left behind, a prayer service was held in the school's auditorium "in which everyone in his or her own way can share in an effort towards the success of the Washington March." In a memo to staff, Dr. Louis Finkelstein, Chancellor of the Seminary, wrote, "I do not have to tell you or anyone else what stress the Jewish religion places on the equality of all human beings and how it regards this as a fundamental religious principle." As part of the service, William Lebeau, a rabbinical student, read selections from Rabbi Heschel's address to the Religion and Race Conference held in Chicago the previous December.

Two hundred fifty thousand people crowded into the Mall in Washington, D.C., on August 28. It was the largest gathering to that date in the nation's capital and was seen by millions more throughout the country over live television. On the platform were the leaders

Thousands gathered in Washington, D.C., for the 1963 "March on Washington." (Archives of Labor and Urban Affairs, Wayne State University)

of the major Jewish-American organizations including
Shad Polier of the American Jewish Congress, Rabbi
Leon Foyer of the Central Conference of American
Rabbis, George Maislan of the United Synagogue of
America, and Rabbi Uri Miller of the Synagogue Council of America. Below them, thousands of other Jews
mingled with other whites and African-Americans.
Delegates of Reform Judaism were conspicuous by the
signs they carried in Hebrew and English bearing the
biblical text from Leviticus inscribed on the Liberty
Bell: "Proclaim liberty throughout the land, and unto
all the inhabitants thereof." Other signs read, "We
march together, Catholics, Jews and Protestants." A
delegation of Conservative Jews marched under the
banner of the United Synagogue of America.

Rabbi Joachim Prinz of the American Jewish Committee was one of two Jewish speakers. His words
stirred the crowd.

"I speak to you as an American Jew.

*As Americans we share the profound concern of
millions of people about the shame and dis-
grace of inequality and injustice which make a
mockery of the great American idea.*

*As Jews we bring to this great demonstration,
in which thousands of us proudly participate, a
two-fold experience—one of the spirit and one
of our history."*

The speaker whose words became etched in America's conscience was Dr. Martin Luther King, Jr. His

stirring "I Have A Dream" speech envisioned an America where "we will be able to speed up that day when all of God's children—black men and white men, Jews and Gentiles, Protestants and Catholics—will be able to join hands and sing in the words of the old Negro spiritual, 'Free at last! Free at last! Thank God

Rabbi Joachim Prinz of the American Jewish Congress shown on television addressing the "March on Washington." (American Jewish Archives)

155

almighty, we are free at last.'" Later that afternoon, Rabbi Prinz joined Martin Luther King, Jr. and a select group of civil rights leaders for a meeting at the White House with President John F. Kennedy.

As Congress debated during the next year, demonstrations against segregation continued. To provide African-Americans with political power, major efforts were placed on voter registration drives in the Deep South. During the "Freedom Summer" of 1964 thousands of college students, professors, and clergy headed to Mississippi. On June 17, a delegation of seventeen rabbis left the convention of the Central Conference of American Rabbis in Atlantic City, New Jersey, and flew to St. Augustine, Florida, at the request of Martin Luther King. King welcomed the rabbis at a church meeting. He told the audience that the rabbis were descended from Moses who led the Jewish people out of slavery and into freedom. "Now," he said, "these rabbis have come here to stand by our side, to witness to our common convictions." The rabbis joined with African-American men, women, and children in protest marches and demonstrations. When they joined in a sit-in at two local restaurants, they were arrested and jailed. As each new group of rabbis was brought in, colleagues already in their cells greeted the newcomers with the Hebrew song of welcome, "Hevaynu Sholom Aleichem" ("We greet you in peace"). For twenty-one hours they were crowded together in the sweltering St. Augustine jail. But their time was not wasted. After reflecting on the reasons that brought them together, they composed a letter which was later widely circulated for its important message.

"We came because we could not stand silently by our brother's blood. We had done that too many times before. We have been vocal in our exhortation of others but the idleness of our hands too often revealed an inner silence.... We came as Jews who remember the millions of faceless people who stood quietly, watching the smoke rise from Hitler's crematoria.... We hope we have strengthened the morale of St. Augustine Negroes as they strive to claim their dignity and humanity; we know they have strengthened ours."

Civil rights activism was not limited to the Deep South. In Baltimore, Maryland, Rabbi Israel Goldman of Congregation Chizuk Amuno was arrested and jailed for leading a demonstration to desegregate a local amusement park. The photograph of the rabbi being fingerprinted at the police station was reprinted in newspapers across the country. Working in shifts, students at the Jewish Theological Seminary and their Protestant neighbors at the Union Theological Seminary left New York to join Roman Catholic seminarians in a continual vigil for civil rights at the Lincoln Memorial in Washington. Assigned to shifts on a round-the-clock schedule, one rabbinical student, one Protestant, and one Roman Catholic seminarian stood silently before the imposing statue of the president who signed the Emancipation Proclamation.

On July 2, 1964, President Lyndon B. Johnson signed into law the Civil Rights Act of 1964. But the

*Martin Luther King, Jr. (left), Rev. Ralph David Abernathy, and
Rabbi Maurice Eisendrath (right).* (American Jewish Archives)

guarantees of the law could not be instantly implemented. During 1964's Freedom Summer, over 1,000
mostly white volunteers in Mississippi set up Freedom
Schools to teach black literature, history, and language
skills. They organized health clinics to bring medical
care to impoverished rural villages. A significant number of those white volunteers were Jewish. Not all
were religiously observant. Many of these "outside agi-
tators" were children of liberal and prosperous families
who themselves never experienced poverty and injustice. A Baltimore rabbi later said in the *Baltimore
Jewish Times*, "Maybe it was naive, but we had a kind

of euphoria that we were changing the world. There was a real affection that transcended racial and religious lives."

On June 21, 1964, three Freedom Summer workers, Andrew Goodman, Michael Schwerner, and James Chaney set out on a drive to Philadelphia, Mississippi. A black church had been burned and the trio was on its way to assist the parishioners. Goodman and Schwerner were Jewish. One was a New York City social worker, the other a college student. Both had come to Mississippi to help. They and Chaney

Michael Schwerner shown on television at a civil rights training session. (Library of Congress)

were never seen alive again. Their disappearance set off a national public outcry. After an intensive FBI investigation, their bodies were found buried in an earthen dam not far from Philadelphia. Each had been shot to death.

The last major demonstration for voting rights took place in March 1965 in Selma, Alabama. Heeding a call from Martin Luther King, Jr. who led the protest, concerned clergy including rabbis arrived to join the marchers. Many of the Jewish students, who made up a large percentage of the white people in the group, came for religious reasons. Others came because it "was the right thing to do." Hundreds of young African-American marchers wore the "Freedom Caps" passed out two years earlier in Birmingham out of respect for the many rabbis who were with them. The rabbis, in turn, conspicuously wore their yarmulkes to identify themselves as Jews, even those Reform rabbis who customarily never wore them.

On March 7, King began a fifty-four-mile march from Selma to Montgomery, the state's capital. The marchers did not get far. As they crossed the Pettus Bridge in Selma, they were met by a phalanx of local and state police who fired tear gas and beat them with nightsticks. The march was halted.

One Protestant minister from Massachusetts was killed and other Freedom Marchers severely injured on that "Bloody Sunday." The major Jewish organizations sent protests to Washington. President Johnson addressed Congress on March 15 and deplored the violence in Selma. "We shall overcome a crippling legacy of bigotry and injustice," he promised and demanded

The disappearance of three young civil rights workers—Goodman, Chaney, and Schwerner—set off one of the largest FBI searches in history. (FBI)

immediate congressional action to eliminate discrimination and allow African-Americans in the South to register and vote.

With federal court authorization and the protection of United States marshals and the National Guard, King regrouped for another attempt on March 21. The eyes of the world focused on Alabama as the marchers proceeded across the bridge. Crowds of angry whites lined the road as cars bearing ugly signs and Confederate flags passed in the opposite direction. Joining King on the march's front line was his friend, Rabbi Heschel, "Father Abraham," a Hawaiian lei bouncing jauntily around his neck. Heschel, aware of the possible dangers, could not stay away and ignore the injustice. Heschel later said, "When I marched with Martin Luther King in Selma, Alabama, I felt my legs were praying." At a mass rally before the Alabama state capitol on March 25, Rabbi Maurice Eisendrath, president of the Union of American Hebrew Congregations was invited by Dr. King to address the crowd.

King was introduced by his associate, the Reverend Ralph David Abernathy. "As God called Joshua to lead His people across the Jordan," Abernathy said, "so also He called Martin Luther King to go to Montgomery and tell Pharaoh Wallace [Alabama's governor], 'Let my people go.'"

On March 25, 1968, just ten days before he was killed by an assassin's bullet, Martin Luther King, Jr. addressed the annual convention of the Rabbinical Assembly. The assembled rabbis greeted King warmly by singing the anthem of the civil rights movement, "We Shall Overcome"—in Hebrew! He was introduced to the gathering of Conservative rabbis by his friend, Abraham Joshua Heschel. "Where does God dwell in America today?" Heschel asked. "Is God at home with those who are complacent, indifferent to other people's agony, devoid of mercy?...Martin Luther King is a sign that God has not forsaken the United States of America. God has sent him to us. His presence is the hope of America. His mission is sacred, his leadership of supreme importance to every one of us....I call upon every Jew to hearken to his advice,

Rabbi Abraham Joshua Heschel marching with Rev. Martin Luther King, Jr. in Selma. (Ratner Center, Jewish Theological Seminary)

163

Marchers cross over the Pettus Bridge in Selma, Alabama, in 1965. (Library of Congress)

to share his vision, to follow in his way. The whole future of America will depend upon the impact and influence of Dr. King."

In turn, Dr. King opened his remarks with praise for Heschel whom he considered "one of the truly great men of our day and age...He is indeed a truly great prophet. All too often the religious community has been a tail light instead of a head light. But here and there we find those who refuse to remain silent behind the safe security of stained glass windows, and they are forever seeking to make the great ethical insights of our

164

Judeo-Christian heritage relevant in this day and in this age. I feel that Rabbi Heschel is one of the persons who is relevant at all times, always standing with prophetic insights to guide us through those difficult days. He has been with us in many of our struggles. I remember marching from Selma to Montgomery, how he stood at my side and with us as we faced that crisis situation."

What followed was an exchange of questions and answers. A wide variety of subjects surfaced including the changing relationship of Jews and African-Americans. "Probably more than any other ethnic group," King said, "the Jewish community has been sympathetic and has stood as an ally to the Negro in his struggle for justice." "On the other hand," he continued, "the Negro confronts the Jew in the ghetto as his landlord in many instances.... I think the only answer to this is for all people to condemn injustice wherever it exists.... I think our responsibility in the black community is to make it very clear that we must never confuse some with all, and certainly in SCLC we have consistently condemned anti-Semitism.... You cannot substitute one tyranny for another, and for the black man to be struggling for justice and then turn around and be anti-Semitic is not only a very irrational course but it is a very immoral course, and wherever we have seen anti-Semitism we have condemned it with all of our might."

Martin Luther King, Jr. was struck down by an assassin's bullet on April 4, 1968. The grieving Rabbi Heschel said, "I think he was one of the greatest prophetic spirits we had in this century.... He brought great blessing to the world—to all of us concerned with the rights of man." Heschel was the only Jew invited to speak at King's funeral service at Morehouse College in Atlanta. When Abraham Joshua Heschel died of a heart condition on December 23, 1972, at age sixty-five, *Newsweek* magazine wrote on his passing, "When the call went out for clerical support of Martin Luther King ...Heschel was the first major Jewish figure to respond and he soon became a fixture at civil rights marches.... Heschel believed that prayer and service are the rewards that God gives those who look to our Creator as Lord."

One religious studies scholar referred to Heschel as "an original thinker with a penetrating and erudite mind...but he was also a champion of the victims of social injustice which was moral scandal and an agent of God's compassion."

10

BUILDING BRIDGES

"The line of progress is never straight."

Martin Luther King, Jr.

Martin Luther King Jr. condemned the rise of anti-Semitism not only before Jewish groups but to blacks. Responding to a letter which read, "I am a Negro, but I don't like Jews," King was forthright. "This is a problem which you need to solve immediately," he wrote, "because it is no different from the attitude that many Whites have concerning the whole Negro race." King echoed the sentiments of his friend, Rabbi Abraham Joshua Heschel, who said, "How many disasters do we have to go through in order to realize that all of humanity has a stake in the liberty of one person; and whenever one person is offended we are all hurt? What begins as the inequality of some inevitably ends as

167

inequality of all." Their words reflect the ongoing quest for equality of all Americans of goodwill.

The modern civil rights struggle evolved through several stages. From 1909 to 1954, the emphasis was on obtaining legal rights. Led by the NAACP, lawyers fought case by case to create a growing collection of legal precedents culminating in the milestone Brown v. Board of Education Supreme Court decision of 1954. From 1955 to 1963, the nation witnessed the power of nonviolent action. When Rosa Parks took a seat at the front of a Montgomery, Alabama bus, she set in motion a series of events which profoundly changed the face of America. The bus boycott that followed thrust Martin Luther King, Jr. into the international spotlight. The 1963 March on Washington demonstrated the resolve of many Americans, black and white, to continue the struggle. These slow and painful steps resulted in the passage of the Civil Rights Act of 1964 and the Voting Rights Bill of 1965. It was a time of great change. Across the country, state legislatures and local communities began to enact enforceable laws to prohibit discrimination in housing and education.

To ensure southern African-Americans of their guaranteed rights, a third phase of the civil rights movement was a concentrated effort to register black voters in the South. Between 1961–1965, young activists from the Student Non-Violent Coordinating Committee (SNCC) and the Congress for Racial Equality (CORE) headed South.

Jews were prominent in the struggle until the onset of the Black Power phase in the mid-1960s. Tired of the slow pace of integration, a new group of civil rights leaders emerged made up of young African-American activists who thrived on confrontation. James Baldwin, the noted African-American writer, explained, "One does not wish, in short, to be told by an American Jew that his suffering was as great as the American Negro's suffering. It isn't and one knows that it isn't from the very tone in which he assures you that it is." White activists, including a large proportion of Jews, were removed from civil rights organization positions. While SNCC and CORE became more militant and less patient with the progress of integration, the Nation of Islam preached hatred against white people and advocated the establishment of a separate black nation in America.

In the midst of this separatist militancy, the National Association for the Advancement of Colored People elected a Jew, Kivie Kaplan, as its president in 1966. Kaplan, a Boston businessman, had long been a civil rights fighter not only in his leadership position within the NAACP but as a lay leader of the Reform wing of American Judaism. He summed up his life-long activism by saying, "thousands of Jews have been killed in pogroms, but for the first time in my life I realized that here were people who were being persecuted in a different way. I felt that, as a Jew, a member of a persecuted group, I should work for other persecuted races...." But Kaplan was to be the last in a long line of Jews who held a leadership role in African-American civil rights groups.

The spirit of cooperation that existed for so long between blacks and Jews weakened considerably after 1966. There was no official break, but each group's

Kivie Kaplan shown at a Chicago demonstration. (American Jewish Archives)

170

conflicting agendas created serious tensions as blacks and Jews became absorbed in their own concerns. For African-Americans, issues such as Black Power and frustration with economic and educational advancement widened the rift. Jews became concerned with issues of Israel and affirmative action.

In 1967, Jews around the world stood by in horror as the combined armies of five Arab countries massed for an attack on Israel designed to "drive the Jews into the sea." Within days, however, the Israelis had turned impending gloom into a stunning military victory. Their crowning glory was the reunification of Jerusalem under Jewish administration. As despair was transformed into relief and joy, American Jews experienced a renewed surge of pride in Israel and a reaffirmation of Jewish life and religion. Black Power advocates did not share American Jews' view of Israel. They considered Israelis to be the oppressors of non-white people who were the victims of "Zionist imperialists" in the Middle East. They compared their own struggle for freedom in the United States with the problems of the Palestinians.

Between 1964 and 1968 over three hundred riots broke out in the black ghettos of major American cities, the result of years of frustration. In the violence, many Jewish-owned stores in ghettos in New York's Harlem; Newark, New Jersey; Detroit, Michigan; and the Watts section of Los Angeles were burned and looted by rampaging mobs. Ironically, these ghettos had been Jewish just a generation earlier. While the Jews had long since moved to suburban homes, many Jewish-owned shops and apartment buildings remained. The only contact

171

most blacks had with Jews was with the shopkeepers and landlords who were trying to keep their small businesses alive. These Jews were the only whites, other than police or firefighters, many African-American ghetto dwellers ever came into contact with in daily life. Very often, that contact resulted in ongoing tensions between ghetto residents and the Jewish landlords and shop owners. That tension, in turn, continued to worsen the relationship of Jews and African-Americans.

In December 1995, a dispute in New York's Harlem between two neighboring businesses, one owned by Jews, the other by African-Americans, ended in violence. After weeks of anti-Semitic demonstrations led by black activists, an armed gunman entered the Jewish-owned store and went on a murderous rampage. The result was the death of eight people—none of them Jewish—and the destruction by fire of both stores. A security guard told police he had earlier overheard a demonstrator saying, "We're going to burn and loot the Jews."

In reaction to the burning of Jewish stores in the 1960s, Martin Luther King wrote in the SCLC newsletter, "As a group, the Jewish citizens of the United States have always stood for freedom, justice and an end to bigotry. . . . Our Jewish friends have demonstrated their commitment to the principle of tolerance and brotherhood in tangible ways, often at great personal sacrifices."

Despite the involvement of Jews in the civil rights movement of the 1960s, historical anti-Semitism was never far from the surface in the black ghetto. The religious reasons for anti-Semitism could be traced back to slave days when African-Americans were first converted to the Christianity of their owners. The noted writer, Richard Wright, graphically described the reason for that hatred when he wrote in *Black Boy*, "All of us black people who lived in the neighborhood hated Jews, not because they exploited us, but because we had been taught at home and in Sunday school that Jews were 'Christ killers.'" Another writer, James Baldwin, said, "Negroes are anti-Semitic because they're anti-white."

Dr. Henry Louis Gates, Jr., the chairperson of Harvard University's Afro-American Studies Department, wrote in *The New York Times* in 1992, "Black anti-Semitism hurts black people first and foremost. In part, because it compromises the moral credibility of our struggle. But equally as important, because it leads us to the politics of distraction, the politics of distortion. ...Anti-Semitism is not going to help us in the struggle against injustice, poverty, AIDS, and violence. So why make excuses for it?"

The decline in relations between the African-American and Jewish communities has been accompanied by a lack of knowledge of the former alliance of both minorities in fighting discrimination in the United States. The era of Martin Luther King, Jr. and Rabbi Abraham Joshua Heschel is gone. The fervor of Rabbi David Einhorn, the leadership of the Spingarns, and the activism of Lillian Wald and Rabbi Stephen S. Wise is largely unknown.

Ms. Carolyn Goodman, mother of Andrew Goodman, the young Jewish college student who was murdered in 1964 together with Michael Schwerner and

James Chaney in Mississippi, said, "I'm more aware than ever of the need for young people to remember the past, to know their history.... The struggle for freedom continues. It must never end." Chaney's brother Ben said, "All of us, blacks and whites, especially blacks and Jews, had a special time when we worked together. But we destroyed that bond. Somehow we have to come back together again, we have to get back to that point."

What motivated the early alliance of Jews and blacks? First and foremost they shared the same vision of America as a country where equal opportunities in all aspects of public life were the right of every American regardless of a person's race or religion. They joined together in liberal causes, believing, as Arnold Forster of the Anti-Defamation League wrote, "racial and religious bigotry cannot thrive in an economically and democratically healthy society." One rabbi, arrested four times in southern civil rights demonstrations in the 1960s said, "I came [to the civil rights movement] because that's what Judaism teaches...that we are all part of the human family." Although the major legal battles were fought and won by 1965, the newly enacted laws did not materially affect the lives of many urban blacks. A new militancy arose that targeted whites in general and Jews specifically.

During the height of the Ocean Hill/Brownsville teacher strike in 1968, which pitted New York City Jewish teachers against African-American community activists, Bayard Rustin, a noted black civil rights leader, put the unleashed hatred against Jews in perspective. "Negro leaders," he stated, "have a moral obligation to fight against anti-Semitism. Jews have been in the forefront of the civil rights fight and probably made more of a contribution than any single group. We cannot be timid and we cannot be silent. Negro children who themselves have been brutalized by racism ought not to be further brutalized by teaching them anti-Semitism and religious prejudice."

In spite of the worsening relations since the mid-1960s, many African-Americans and Jews have sought to create racial peace. Both groups, as minorities in a pluralistic America, shared common interests. In 1969, a biracial committee in New York put advertisements in newspapers asking readers, "Shall we split into warring tribes or unite in solving the problem?" Each group has its own view of America. Author Letty Cottin Pogrebin wrote, "To Blacks, America is the nation that enslaved them and continues to deny them opportunities. To Jews, it is a promised land that makes good on its promises. Blacks worry that their bad situation will never improve; Jews worry that our good situation will not last."

In a 1994 speech before a Jewish leadership conference, Congressman Kweisi Mfume of Maryland, the chairperson of the Congressional Black Caucus who the following year became president of the National Association for the Advancement of Colored People, spoke of the need for cooperation. "Clearly," he said, "there are points both sides could make, but the future of both communities must not be seen as a debate point."

"Our interests are as strongly allied as they have ever been," the president of the American Jewish Committee said at a 1990 meeting. Benjamin Hooks, the

African-American civil rights leader, spoke at the same meeting. "We have to have allies," he said. "Hatred doesn't get you anywhere." Shortly after her 1995 election as chairperson of the National Association for the Advancement of Colored People, Ms. Myrlie Evers Williams spoke of the need to heal the rift between blacks and Jews. She recalled "the time when there was a Kivie Kaplan and others, who were as devoted to the NAACP as I am today." Ms. Williams is the widow of Medgar Evers, the head of the Mississippi branch of the NAACP murdered by a white supremacist in 1963.

A lasting tradition, begun in 1969, has been joint Passover sedarim between Jewish and African-American groups. Drawing upon African-American reverence for the biblical story of the Exodus of the Jews from Egypt, Jews and blacks across America gather yearly to retell the story of freedom. In cities across America, the American Jewish Congress brings Jews and African-Americans together to honor Martin Luther King, Jr.'s birthday. "We are trying on a one-to-one basis," an American Jewish Congress official said, "to bring children together." Another added, "It's a way to rekindle the warm feeling that existed between blacks and Jews during the civil rights movement. The purpose is to tear down the wall of discrimination."

Programs that bring together African-American and Jewish students offer further hope for reconciliation. "The Black-Jewish fight is an adult thing," said a minister in Boston where the Jewish community established the Jewish InterAction program for teenagers. Five projects focus on the city's black neighborhoods. The director of Boston's Jewish Community Relations

176

Council explained that the projects "are very concrete, so as to reestablish contact," so individuals may "get to know each other, and reduce alienation." One of the Boston projects is called "Boston Freedom Summer" based on the goals of the 1964 Freedom Summer in Mississippi which attracted hundreds of young Jewish volunteers.

In Philadelphia, "Operation Understanding," established in 1985 by the American Jewish Committee and the Urban League, trains selected African-American and Jewish high school students in each other's culture and traditions. In a three-phase program, which includes trips to Israel and Africa's Republic of Senegal, students form strong bonds of friendship with each other. They then go out into their respective communities to educate others. The experience profoundly affects the participants. One African-American student wrote, "Racism and anti-Semitism grow from the same root. . . . our distances are bound up in common tears and in common pain." A Jewish student remarked, "The first step toward change is communication. It is only through dialogue that we can learn about each other and learn to appreciate each other. Only through dialogue can we begin to break down stereotypes."

In other cities, meetings of African-American and Jewish students explore different ways young people can help society achieve racial harmony. Under the sponsorship of B'nai B'rith and local businesses and organizations, "A World of Understanding" programs to combat discrimination and bigotry annually involve thousands of young people. In Washington, D.C., "Operation Understanding D.C." links white and black high school students. One participant said, "It made me realize that it's not about me all the time. It's not about one group, but about all working together."

A special exhibition, "Bridges and Boundaries: African-Americans and American Jews," was created in 1993 by The Jewish Museum in New York in collaboration with the National Association for the Advancement of Colored People. Joan Rosenbaum, the museum's director, spoke of the exhibition as a way to present "a new understanding of the ethnic identities of African-Americans and American Jews, and new inspiration for reaching out to each other and continuing the dialogue." From New York, the exhibit traveled to other museums across the country. In Philadelphia, it was the central focus of social, cultural, and musical activities at the Afro-American Historical and Cultural Museum and the National Museum of American Jewish History bringing together people of both communities.

Murray Friedman, former vice chairperson of the United States Civil Rights Commission, said in a 1995 speech that "We cannot recreate the black-Jewish alliance. The issue now is one of normalizing the relationship. We have to get beyond the romanticism [of the civil rights movement] and to the practical." Ten years earlier, Vernon E. Jordan, Jr., the long-time leader of the National Urban League, said, "There will be plenty of things that blacks and Jews will disagree about. That should be accepted as a given. There will also be plenty that we can agree upon, and it is upon those issues that we should reconstitute our historic alliance."

A cooperative venture of Boston's African-American business community and the American Jewish Committee provides support to the city's black business owners. The Black-Jewish Economic Roundtable was the idea of Dr. Lawrence Lowenthal, the area director of the American Jewish Committee. "My interest as a director of a human relations organization," Lowenthal said, "is enhancing relations between the black and Jewish community. The most effective way we can do that at this time is to foster economic cooperation."

These cooperative ventures mark the beginning of a serious effort to reconcile differences between Jews and African-Americans. Before the healing process is complete, blacks and Jews must better appreciate their intertwined civil rights history and work to eliminate the mindless anti-Jewish hatred that exists in parts of the African-American community.

Speaking before the World Jewish Congress in 1994, Coretta Scott King, continuing the work of her late husband, spoke out against anti-Semitism. "Just as Jewish leaders have condemned racism, like Martin Luther King, Jr., I feel I have a moral obligation to deplore the expressions of anti-Semitism that have polluted our society." Then, she quoted from her late husband's speech before the Rabbinical Assembly just ten days before he was killed. "Anti-Semitism is as vile and contemptible as racism," Dr. King said. "Anyone who supports it, including African-Americans, does a disservice to his people, his country and his God." Ms. King concluded with her own words: "With this faith and this commitment, together, we shall overcome. Shalom, and God bless you all."

A TIMELINE OF KEY EVENTS, 1619–1968

From the Arrival of the First Jews and Blacks in America to the Assassination of Martin Luther King, Jr.

1619 First boatload of African slaves arrives in Jamestown, Virginia.

1654 First Jewish settlers arrive in New Amsterdam.

1791 The First Amendment to the United States Constitution guarantees equality to all Americans.

1824 Passage of Maryland's "Jew Bill" granting Jews the right to hold elective office.

1843 B'nai B'rith founded.

1848 Arrival of large number of Jews from Germany.

1851 Ernestine Rose, a Polish-born Jewish woman, captivates audiences with her speeches against slavery and for women's rights.

1856 August Bondi rides with John Brown in Kansas, fighting pro-slavery forces.

1861 Rabbi David Einhorn vigorously denounces the pro-slavery remarks of Rabbi Morris Raphall.

1861–1865 Civil War.

1881 Tennessee is first state to establish "Jim Crow" railroad laws, which are quickly adopted by other southern states.

1881 Beginning of massive Jewish immigration from Eastern Europe.

1893 Lillian Wald founds the Henry Street Settlement in New York.

1896 The United States Supreme Court upholds the doctrine of "separate but equal" in Plessy v. Ferguson.

1906 Founding of the American Jewish Committee.

1909 Founding of the National Association for the Advancement of Colored People (NAACP).

1911 National Urban League (NUL) founded.

1913 Founding of the Anti-Defamation League (ADL) by B'nai B'rith to combat anti-Semitism.

1915–1930 The Great Migration of African-Americans to northern cities.

1915 Lynching of Leo Frank in Georgia.

1917 Julius Rosenwald Fund chartered.

1918 Rabbi Stephen S. Wise founds the American Jewish Congress.

1926 A. Philip Randolph founds the Brotherhood of Sleeping Car Porters.

1929 Joel E. Spingarn elected president of the NAACP.

1939 Arthur Spingarn succeeds his brother, Joel, as NAACP president.

1945 Rabbi Abraham Joshua Heschel joins the faculty of the Jewish Theological Seminary of America.

1947 President Truman's Committee on Civil Rights issues its report, "To Secure These Rights."

1954 United States Supreme Court reverses "separate but equal" doctrine in the case of Brown v. Board of Education.

1955 Ms. Rosa Parks arrested in Montgomery, Alabama. Bus boycott propels Dr. Martin Luther King, Jr. into forefront of the civil rights movement.

1958 Bombings of temples in the South.

1960 "Sit-ins" begin at the Woolworth lunch counter in Greensboro, North Carolina.

1961 Freedom Riders test federal desegregation orders for interstate transportation.

1963 March on Washington.

1963 Civil rights demonstrations in Birmingham, Alabama.

1964 Passage of the Civil Rights Act forbidding discrimination in public accommodations and employment.

1964 Three young civil rights workers, Goodman, Schwerner, and Chaney, murdered in Philadelphia, Mississippi, during "Freedom Summer."

1965 Martin Luther King, Jr. awarded Nobel Peace Prize. Demonstrations in Selma, Alabama.

1968 Assassination of Dr. Martin Luther King, Jr.

NOTES

CHAPTER ONE

Page 1   "who caught and killed Nat Turner . . . Jews! Jews!" Richard Cohen, "A Nasty Night at Howard," *The Washington Post*, 1 March 1994, p. A9.

Page 2   "Nobody could have imagined . . . because he was Jewish." *Newsday*, 11 June 1992, p. 7.

Page 4   "I was a prisoner . . . my children have been traumatized." *New York*, 11 January, 1993.

Page 6   "Twenty-three Jews . . . at least one slave." Howard Brackman, *Ministry of Lies*, (New York: Four Walls Eight Windows, 1994), 75.

Page 8   "In the 1960s . . . turned the strike ugly." Jerald E. Podair, *The Failure to See*, (Philadelphia: The Center for American Jewish History and the American Jewish Committee, 1992).

CHAPTER TWO

Page 15   "The Jews, Stuyvesant and . . . and unbelieving Jews." Bernard Schwartz, *Behind Bakke,* (New York: New York University Press, 1988), 128.

Page 18   "We have seen and learned . . . to that of equal citizen." Norman H. Finkelstein, *The Other 1492: Jewish Settlement in the New World,* (New York: Scribners, 1989), chap. 8.

CHAPTER THREE

Page 24   "Perhaps nothing did more . . . the underground railroad." John Hope Franklin, *From Slavery to Freedom,* (New York: Knopf, 1967), 189.

Page 26   "The Jews of the United States . . . friends of universal freedom." Louis Ruchames, "The Abolitionists and the Jews," *Publications of the American Jewish Historical Society,* 42 (September 1953):154.

Page 27   "I am an example . . . her eloquence is irresistible." Jayme Sokolow, "Revolution and Reform: The Antebellum Jewish Abolitionists," *Journal of Ethnic Studies* 9, no. 1 (Spring 1981):36.

Page 27   "a female . . . parents in Poland." Alberta Eiseman, *Rebels and Reformers,* (New York: Zenith Books, 1976), 54.

Page 28   "I am most anxious . . . reason condemned them." Leon Huhner, "Some Jewish Associates of John Brown," *Publications of the American Jewish Historical Society* 5 (1897):151.

Page 33   "At the same time . . . backward social customs and traditions." Jayme Sokolow, "Revolution and Reform: The Antebellum Jewish Abolitionists," *Journal of Ethnic Studies* 9, no. 1 (Spring, 1981):34.

Page 34   "uttered burning words . . . him from speaking." Max Kohler, "Jews and the American Anti-Slavery Movement," *Publications of the American Jewish Historical Society* 5 (1897):151.

Page 39   "repeatedly denounced slavery . . . his moving eloquence." Letter from Rabbi Charles A. Rubenstein, February 15, 1945, from the files of the Jewish Historical Society of Maryland.

Page 39   "at least a large portion . . . at the proper time." *American Jewish Archives*, (November 1961):153.

CHAPTER FOUR

Page 42   "My mother . . . a brief period." Lenora Berson, *The Negroes and the Jews*, (New York: Random House, 1971), 66.

Page 49 "It seems incredible . . . citizen of this country." Playthell Benjamin, "African Americans and Jews: A Tattered Alliance," *Emerge* (October 1990):75.

Page 51 "convinced many Jews . . . in the United States." Yvonne DeCarlo Newsome, "A House Divided," (Ph. D. diss., Northwestern University, 1991), 80.

Page 52 "refugees from the 'two Souths' . . . on the banks of the Hudson." Harold Brackman, "The Ebb and Flow of Conflict: A History of Black-Jewish Relations Through 1900," (Ph.D. diss., University of California at Los Angeles, 1977), 414.

Page 53 "contribute our sense of citizenship . . . democratic society." Alberta Eiseman, *Rebels and Reformers,* (New York: Zenith Books, 1976), 107.

Page 53 "abolishment of separate schools . . . social and racial prejudice." Harold Brackman, "The Ebb and Flow of Conflict: A History of Black-Jewish Relations Through 1900," (Ph.D. diss., University of California at Los Angeles, 1977), 339.

Page 56 "It may be too early . . . this is his achievement." Letter from Rabbi Stephen S. Wise to Sara Howell, January 1943, The Stephen S. Wise Papers, American Jewish Historical Society.

Page 58   "involvement with the NAACP . . . and race riots." Robert Shapiro, "A Reform Rabbi in the Progressive Era: The Early Career of Stephen S. Wise," (Ph. D. diss., Harvard University, 1984), 298.

CHAPTER FIVE

Page 61   "We commit ourselves . . . attend no meeting." B. Joyce Ross, *J. E. Spingarn and the Rise of the NAACP,* (New York: Atheneum, 1972), 55.

Page 61   "We had on our board . . . and radical Negroes." Yvonne DeCarlo Newsome, "A House Divided," (Ph. D. diss., Northwestern University, 1991), 128.

Page 63   "It is possible . . . in this country." B. Joyce Ross, *J. E. Spingarn and the Rise of the NAACP,* (New York: Atheneum, 1972), 26.

Page 64   "We white men of whatever creed . . . own leaders and your own money." B. Joyce Ross, *J. E. Spingarn and the Rise of the NAACP,* (New York: Atheneum, 1972), 26.

Page 64   "The real danger . . . to convert white people." Letter from J. E. Spingarn to James Weldon Johnson, June 27, 1921, *NAACP Papers,* Library of Congress.

Page 65   "prepare as soon as possible . . . grounds of our objection." Letter from J. E. Spingarn, March 17, 1915, *NAACP Papers*, Library of Congress.

Page 68   "The situation of the Negroes . . . we Jews experienced." Hasia Diner, *In the Almost Promised Land: American Jews and Blacks, 1915–1935*, (Westport: Greenwood, 1977), 76.

Page 68   "I belong to an ancient race . . . not going to give up." Hasia Diner, *In The Almost Promised Land: American Jews and Blacks, 1915–1935*, (Westport: Greenwood, 1977), 151–52.

Page 69   "The Civil Rights Act . . . is not involved." Letter from Arthur Spingarn, March 4, 1929, *NAACP Papers*, Library of Congress.

Page 70   "The moment that there is . . . have been shattered." Murray Friedman, *What Went Wrong: The Creation and Collapse of the Black-Jewish Alliance*, (New York: Free Press, 1995), 70.

Page 72   "I do not believe . . . principles and opinions." B. Joyce Ross, *J. E. Spingarn and the Rise of the NAACP*, (New York: Atheneum, 1972), 85.

Page 73   "A new sense . . . self-respect together." Letter from J. E. Spingarn to James Weldon Johnson, June 27, 1921, *NAACP Papers*, Library of Congress.

CHAPTER SIX

Page 78 "Whether it is because . . . for the colored race." *American Jewish Yearbook,* (Philadelphia: The Jewish Publication Society, 1932), 160.

Page 81 "Where we was going . . . in a black school." Thomas Hanchett, "The Rosenwald Schools and Black Education in North Carolina," *The North Carolina Historical Review* 65 (4):421.

Page 83 "most influential philanthropic . . . social conditions change." Thomas Hanchett, *The North Carolina Historical Review* 65 (4):426.

Page 83 "The Negro does not . . . segregation is outlawed." Thomas Hanchett, *The North Carolina Historical Review* 65 (4):425.

CHAPTER SEVEN

Page 90 "It must have appeared . . . on American crime." John P. Roche, *The Quest for the Dream,* (New York: Macmillan, 1963), 93.

Page 92 "At no time in American history . . . Congress in the news." *Congress Bulletin* 8, no.7 (1940):7.

Page 92 "I want to make it plain . . . at present obtain." David Brody, "American Jewry, the Refugees and Immigration (1932–1942)," vol. 5 of *The Jewish Experience in America,*

(Waltham: The American Jewish Historical Society, 1969), 332.

Page 95   "During the election . . . mark for enemies." *B'nai B'rith Magazine,* 51 (November 1936): 43.

Page 107   "We had won . . . and grade schools." Jack Greenberg, *Crusaders in the Courts,* (New York: Basic Books, 1994), 81.

CHAPTER EIGHT

Page 113   "If we don't rise . . . democratic authority of the land." P. Allen Krause, "Rabbis and Negro Rights in the South, 1954–1970," *American Jewish Archive,* 21, no. 1 (April 1969):33.

CHAPTER NINE

Page 129   "I've learned from the prophets . . . prophets are unknown." Abraham Joshua Heschel interview, *The Eternal Light,* NBC Television Network, 4 February 1973.

Page 129   "The Negro movement . . . to answer God's demand." Abraham Joshua Heschel, *The Insecurity of Freedom,* (New York: Noonday Press, 1967), 110.

Page 130   "It was easier for the . . . United States Senate." Abraham Joshua Heschel, *The Insecurity of Freedom*, (New York: Noonday Press, 1967), 103.

Page 130   "Equality as religious commandment . . . a Negro is disfranchised." Harold Kasimow and Byron Sherwin, eds., *No Religion Is An Island*, (Maryknoll: Orbis, 1991), 90.

Page 130   "Can you imagine . . . against human beings." Susannah Heschel, "My Father: Abraham Joshua Heschel," *Present Tense*, 14, no. 3 (March/April 1987):49.

Page 131   "Daily we should . . . to prevent humiliation." Abraham Joshua Heschel, *The Insecurity of Freedom*, (New York: Noonday Press, 1967), 98.

Page 135   Albert Vorspan, "In St. Augustine," *Midstream*, (September, 1964):15–22.

Page 137   "The last major demonstration . . . right thing to do." Seymour Siegel, "Pilgrimage to Selma," *Congress Bi-Weekly*, (29 March, 1965):5–6.

Page 140   "Probably more than . . . with all of our night." "Conversation With Martin Luther King," *Conservative Judaism*, 22, no 3 (Spring 1968):1–19.

CHAPTER TEN

Page 148 "I came [to the civil rights movement] . . . the human family." *Newsday*, 29 November 1988, p. 15.

Page 148 "Negro leaders, he stated . . . and religious prejudice." *The New York Times*, 9 January 1969.

SELECTED BIBLIOGRAPHY

BOOKS

Archer, Jules. *They Had A Dream*. New York: Viking, 1993 (young adult title).

Berman, Paul, ed. *Blacks and Jews*. New York: Delacorte, 1994.

Berson, Lenora. *The Negroes and the Jews*. New York: Random House, 1971 (out of print).

Brackman, Harold. *Ministry of Lies*. New York: Four Walls Eight Windows, 1994.

Branch, Taylor. *Parting the Waters*. New York: Simon and Schuster, 1988.

Cohen, Naomi. *Not Free to Desist: A History of the American Jewish Committee, 1906–1966*. Philadelphia: Jewish Publication Society, 1972 (out of print).

Diner, Hasia. *In the Almost Promised Land: American Jews and Blacks, 1915–1935*. Westport: Greenwood, 1977.

Dudley, Mark. *Brown v. Board of Education*. New York: Twenty-First Century Books, 1994 (young adult title).

Eiseman, Alberta. *Rebels and Reformers*. New York: Zenith, 1976 (young adult title; out of print).

Forster, Arnold. *A Measure of Freedom*. New York: Doubleday, 1950 (out of print).

Friedman, Murray. *What Went Wrong? The Creation and Collapse of the Black-Jewish Alliance*. New York: Free Press, 1995.

Greenberg, Jack. *Crusaders in the Courts.* New York: Basic, 1994.

Haskins, James. *Freedom Rides.* New York: Hyperion, 1995 (young adult title).

Heschel, Abraham J. *The Insecurity of Freedom.* New York: Noonday Press, 1967.

Kaufman, Jonathan. *Broken Alliance.* New York: Scribners, 1988.

Kellogg, Charles. *NAACP: A History.* Baltimore: Johns Hopkins University Press, 1967.

Korn, Bertram. *American Jewry and the Civil War.* Philadelphia: Jewish Publication Society, 1951 (out of print).

Lerner, Michael, and West, Cornel. *Jews and Blacks.* New York: Putnam, 1995.

Lester, Julius. *Lovesong: Becoming a Jew.* New York: Holt, 1988.

Lewis, David Levering. *W.E.B. Du Bois.* New York: Holt, 1994.

McKissack, Patricia and Frederick. *The Civil Rights Movement in America.* Chicago: Children's Press, 1987 (young adult title).

Merkle, John C., ed. *Abraham Joshua Heschel.* New York: Macmillan, 1985.

Powledge, Fred. *We Shall Overcome.* New York: Scribners, 1993 (young adult title).

Roche, John P. *The Quest for the Dream.* New York: Macmillan, 1963.

Ross, B. Joyce. *J.E. Spingarn and the Rise of the NAACP.* New York: Atheneum, 1972 (out of print).

Salzman, Jack, ed. *Bridges and Boundaries.* New York: Braziller, 1992.

Sherwin, Byron. *Abraham Joshua Heschel.* Atlanta: John Knox Press, 1979.

Sorin, Gerald. *A Time for Building.* Baltimore: The Johns Hopkins University Press, 1992.

Vorspan, Albert. *Giants of Justice.* New York: Union of American Hebrew Congregations, 1960 (young adult title; out of print).

Weisbord, Robert. *Bittersweet Encounter.* Westport: Negro Universities Press, 1970 (out of print).

Weisbrot, Robert. *Marching Toward Freedom.* New York: Chelsea House, 1994 (young adult title).

ARTICLES

Angell, Pauline. "Julius Rosenwald," *American Jewish Year Book 5673.* 34(1932).

Blauner, Bob. "That Black-Jewish Thing: What's Going On?" *Tikkun.* 9 (Sept-Oct 1994).

———. "Conversation With Martin Luther King." *Conservative Judaism.* 22, no.3 (Spring 1968).

Dresner, Samuel. "The Contribution of Abraham Joshua Heschel." *Judaism.* 32, no.125 (Winter 1983).

Einhorn, David. "A Farewell to Baltimore." *American Jewish Archives.* 13 (November 1961).

Friedman, Murray. "Jews, Blacks, and the Civil Rights Revolution." *New Perspectives.* 17, no.4 (Fall 1985).

Getlin, Josh. "A Burning Legacy." *Los Angeles Times,* 15 June 1989, p.1.

Hanchett, Thomas. "The Rosenwald Schools and Black Education in North Carolina." *The North Carolina Historical Review.* 65, no.4, (October 1988).

Huhner, Leon. "Some Jewish Associates of John Brown." *Publications of the American Jewish Historical Society.* 23 (1915).

Jordan, Vernon. "Blacks and Jews: What Went Wrong." *Washington Post.* 15 June 1984, p. 23.

Kohler, Max J. "Jews and the American Anti-Slavery Movement II." *Publications of the American Jewish Historical Society.* 9 (1901).

Mills, David. "Half-Truths and History: The Debate Over Jews and Slavery." *Washington Post.* 17 October 1993, p. C3.

Ovington, Mary. "How the National Association for the Advancement of Colored People Began." *Crisis.* 91, no.2 (February 1984).

Ruchames, Louis. "The Abolitionists and the Jews." *Publications of the American Jewish Historical Society.* 62 (September 1953).

Shankman, Arnold. "A Temple Is Bombed-Atlanta, 1958." *American Jewish Archives.* 23, no.2 (November 1971).

Sokolow, Jayme. "Revolution and Reform: The Antebellum Jewish Abolitionists." *Journal of Ethnic Studies.* 9, no.1 (Spring 1981).

Ungar, Andre. "To Birmingham, and Back." *Conservative Judaism.* 18, no.1 (Fall 1963).

Wieseltier, Leon et al. "The Rift Between Blacks and Jews." *Time.* 143, 28 February 1994.

OTHER SOURCES

The Papers of the National Association for the Advancement of Colored People, 1909–1939. The Library of Congress, Washington.

The Records of the American Jewish Committee. YIVO Institute, New York.

The Records of the American Jewish Congress. American Jewish Historical Society, Brandeis University Campus, Waltham, Massachusetts.

The Papers of Rabbi Stephen S. Wise. American Jewish Historical Society, Brandeis University Campus, Waltham, Massachusetts.

The Records of the Jewish Theological Seminary of America, New York.

INDEX

Note: An *i* after a page number indicates an illustration or photograph.